The Life of the Fields

José Antonio Muñoz Rojas

The Life of the Fields
Las cosas del campo

Translated from Spanish by
Andrew Dempsey & Álvaro García

Shearsman Books

First published in the United Kingdom in 2024 by
Shearsman Books
P.O. Box 4239
Swindon
SN3 9FN

Shearsman Books Ltd Registered Office
30–31 St. James Place, Mangotsfield, Bristol BS16 9JB
(this address not for correspondence)

www.shearsman.com

ISBN 978-1-84861-950-0

Copyright © José Antonio Muñoz Rojas, 1999
Copyright © Pre-Textos, 1999
Translations copyright © Andrew Dempsey & Álvaro García, 2024

The right of Andrew Dempsey & Álvaro García to be identified as the translators of this work has been asserted in accordance with the Copyrights, Designs and Patents Act of 1988.
All rights reserved.

ACKNOWLEDGEMENTS

Las cosas del campo was first published in 1951 by El Arroyo de los Ángeles, Málaga. The most recent edition, in 1999, is from Editorial Pre-Textos, Valencia, whose permission to publish this translation we gratefully acknowledge.

We thank also the representatives of the author's Estate for supporting this project.

Cover photograph: Juan Miguel Pando Barrero (1915–1992) from the archive of the Instituto del Patrimonio Cultural de España, Ministerio de Cultura.

CONTENTS

	Preface and Acknowledgements	7
	Author's Foreword	9

I

16	Las puertas del campo / Gates on the Land	17
18	Llegan los abejarucos / The Bee-eaters Arrive	19
20	Primeras noticias / Early Signs	21
22	Sazón de todo / Everything Has Its Season	23
24	Las yerbas ignoradas / Neglected Grasses	25
26	Las herrizas / Stony Hillsides	27
28	Miguelillo el pavero / Miguelillo Who Minds the Turkeys	29
30	Cuando florecen las encinas / When the Holm Oaks Flower	31
32	Narciso el cantor / Narciso the Singer	33
34	Las lilas / Lilacs	35
36	Las rejas enlutadas / Ploughshares in Mourning	37
38	Las amazonas / Amazons	39
42	Las nubes / Clouds	43

II

46	Las gayombas / Yellow Broom	47
48	Los jaramagos / Charlock	49
50	Las tórtolas / Turtle Doves	51
52	Juanillo / Juanillo	53
56	Los álamos blancos / White Poplars	57
58	El verano / Summer	59
60	La barcina / Harvesting	61
62	Los instrumentos del verano / The Implements of Summer	63
64	El velador / Night Guardian	65
66	Los melonares / The Melon Beds	67
68	El solano / The Solano	69
70	La risa de dolores / The Laughter of Dolores	71
72	Hombres del campo / Men of the Fields	73

III

76	La matalahúga / Anise	77
78	Los verdes / Greens	79
80	La pájara / The Hen Bird	81
82	Los olivos / The Olive Trees	83
84	La flauta / Flauta	85
86	Los trigos / Wheat	87
88	Nicolás el historiador / Nicolás the Historian	89
90	El primer soplo del otoño / The First Breath of Autumn	91
92	Miguelillo se va / Miguelillo Is Going Away	93
94	Los rastrojos arden / The Stubble Is Burning	95
96	Se cae la aceituna / The Olives Are Falling	97
98	El pensador / The Stable Boy	99

IV

102	El corazón y el campo / The Heart and the Country	103
104	Los aceituneros / The Olive Pickers	105
106	Labranza / Working the Land	107
108	El ojiblancar / The Old Olive Grove	109
110	El talador / The Pruner of the Olive Trees	111
112	Las heladas / Frosts	113
114	Finales de enero / Late January	115
116	Los zorzales no vienen / The Thrushes Are Not Coming	117
118	Los mulos / The Mules	119
120	Tornan los abejarucos / The Bee-eaters Are Back	121
122	Las abejas en los tilos / The Bees in the Lime Trees	123
124	Tierra eterna / Eternal Earth	125

Author's Introduction, 1976	127
Author's Afterword, 1999	129
Translators' Note	130
Biographical Notes	131

PREFACE AND ACKNOWLEDGEMENTS

This book is about the people and the landscape of Andalusia at a specific time, in the middle of the last century, still recognisable, still to be found, despite the fact that Andalusia has seen so many changes in these past seventy years. The book was inspired by the landscape around the family home of the Spanish poet José Antonio Muñoz Rojas (1909–2009) near the country town of Antequera in the province of Málaga. It is about the country house and farm, the Casería del Conde, and the people who lived and worked there. But it has come to be seen as representing a whole epoch of rural Andalusia and is full of magical descriptions of the land and its people, their character and ways of life. The interest and regard the English have always shown for Andalusia is justification enough for bringing this most attractive book into our language.

Muñoz Rojas is one of the finest but least known poets of his generation. He was an Anglophile with a very considerable knowledge of English literature. He translated Shakespeare, Wordsworth, Hopkins, Eliot and others. In 1936 he was in Cambridge beginning a thesis on the relationship between the English 'metaphysical' poets and those of the Spain's 'golden age'. These studies were interrupted by the Spanish Civil War which began that summer. His Cambridge connections and the part they played in his near-death experiences in the first months of the war are recounted in his memoir *La Gran Musaraña*, published in 1994.

As well as *Las cosas del campo*, two books of poetry by Muñoz Rojas are especially celebrated, *Cantos a Rosa*, 1954, love songs of lyrical and intricate form; and *Objetos perdidos*, 1997, a book of discreet humour about the trials of old age and religious devotion for which he received Spain's National Poetry Prize. In the post-war years Muñoz Rojas worked for the Banco Urquijo in Madrid. In those difficult years he helped many poets whether or not they were in favour with the Franco regime.

Las cosas del campo has been published and re-published over a period of fifty years, in Málaga, Madrid and Valencia – in three cities and indeed for three appreciative generations.

We have translated *Las cosas del campo* as 'The Life of the Fields' (with acknowledgement to that great writer on nature and life, Richard Jefferies). Behind the original title lies the phrase of the Roman poet Lucretius, *De rerum natura*. *Las cosas del campo* was first published in 1951 in Málaga in a small edition. It is regarded as one of the finest twentieth-century books of prose poetry in the Spanish language. Muñoz Rojas gives an account of how the book and its publication came about in his two prefaces to editions in 1951 and 1976 which are reprinted here together with an afterword from the edition published by Pre-Textos in 1999. It is the text of this last edition which we have followed for this translation, with grateful acknowledgements to the publishers and to the family of José Antonio Muñoz Rojas.

The poet Vicente Aleixandre (1898–1984), in correspondence with Muñoz Rojas, referred to the language of this book as 'tan aparentemente sencilla y tan difícil', so apparently simple and so difficult. The vocabulary is at once subtle and magical to a high degree, even to the limit of what is translatable, and also, or even primarily, specific to its time and place. Many of the words and even what they describe belong to another era. Yet through poetry the book transcends its references and enters into the realms of spirit and mystery, humour and love.

We thank the many people who have helped in the long process of preparing this book, most especially the poet's daughter Gracia Muñoz Bayo and her husband Rafael Mazarrasa; Manuel Borrás and Manuel Ramírez of the publishing house Pre-Textos, which has done so much to bring the poetry and prose of Muñoz Rojas into the canon of Spanish letters; Tim Chapman, Josefa Lebron Molinillo, Mark Haworth-Booth, Alister Warman and Catherine Lampert.

Andrew Dempsey & Álvaro García

AUTHOR'S FOREWORD

I know something of this land and its people. I know it in its gentleness and in its harshness, I have followed its paths, and I have rested my eyes on its beauty. I close them now and have it in front of me; an ungiving land, the soil dry and sandy; a few fertile fields and large expanses of red earth; here the ridges of a hill, there the hollow of a ravine; a vista of dusty terrain, the beating wings of a bustard in slow flight. The whole landscape is in unhurried flight. The stony hillsides are crowned with shrub oaks, and here and there a solitary holm oak sings its story. Such lonely holm oaks are the teeth left in the land, to record sonorous hills with great oaks and many rockroses, with scattered shade and places where no one has trodden, a time when animal life reigned supreme and springtime was freedom.

Today... today the landscape says it clearly: arable land up to this point and from here the beginning of pasture. Holm oaks have a two-thousand-year history, olives barely a hundred. And the olives, ash green or silver, changing with the wind, how much they resemble the sea, in their order, in their monotony. How much blood has been shed on this land! Not red blood not spilt blood, but the blood of the labourer, of sweat and tears. So many dreams, so much hope is expressed in these field borders, so seemingly haphazard but in truth so close to poetry! So much rich humanity!

I tremble going through these pastures, crossing the edges of these fields, climbing these hillsides. I feel strangely eternal. I immerse myself in this land, my spirit relishes so much bitterness, so much sweetness, invested in these yearly furrows and sown fields. Year in year out, man persists, tied to this land, from sun to sun, from furrow to furrow, burying himself in it. We walk over his sweat, over his illusions, over his bones. That is why I tremble a little as I go through these fields, through this incantation. And I am afraid I will not to be able to complete what I have begun. Wherever one begins, it will never reach its end. My song will remain in the middle of the journey, still on my lips. But the land will continue the song. The larks and the curlews will hear it; a smuggler out late on these footpaths, someone who has lost their way amongst the olives; lovers seeking the complicity of the night and the hard earth to offer their love. Oh song, as useless and as necessary as this immense profusion of wildflowers every year!

Casería del Conde, 1946

LAS COSAS DEL CAMPO

A mis hermanos

THE LIFE OF THE FIELDS

For my brothers

I

I

LAS PUERTAS DEL CAMPO

Quién sabe las razones de un amor? Son secretas como las aguas bajo la tierra, que luego salen en manantial donde menos se espera. Nada se guarda y el amor menos que nada. A fuerza de pasar los ojos sobre este campo, lo vamos conociendo como el cuerpo de una enamorada, distinguimos todas sus señales, sabemos la ocasión del gozo, la de la esquivez. ¡Oh enorme cuerpo del amante! Por tus barrancos y por tus veras, por tus graciosos cielos, por tus caminos, ya polvorientos, ya encharcados, por tus rincones ocultos y tus abiertas extensiones, por agostos y por eneros, te he cabalgado. Tu también conoces los cascos de mi caballo. En la más dura coscoja, en la matilla más oculta, en vuelo y en terrón, en todo te he buscado.

Eres un río de hermosura pasando, sonando, ajustándote a la noche, al día, a la estación. Por ti siento pasos antiguos, correr sangre de esta misma de mis venas. Todos somos como tú, algo que ni empieza ni acaba, como la hermosura o estos olivares cuyo fin nunca alcanzan mis ojos.

Y esperamos. A veces es algo áspero este roce del corazón. Todo por fuera está inmutable y algo por dentro roza. ¿Que será? Un gran aletazo del amor nos sacará a su luz. Quedará todo limpio. Allá en nuestro rinconcillo, el amor sigue. Oh campo, esta hermosura no tiene página ni espejo y sólo, a veces, se deja seducir por el temblor de la palabra, por la insinuación de la poesía. Pero, ¿recogerte, encerrarte? ¿Quién pone puertas al campo?

GATES ON THE LAND *

Who knows the reasons for love? They are as secret as the waters under the earth which spring up where least expected. Nothing is fixed and love least of all. As a consequence of looking so often over this land we are coming to know it like the body of a loved one, aware of its intimations, knowing the moment for engaging and the moment for holding back. Oh, Lover's immense body! I have ridden through your ravines and your slopes, under your clement skies, on your paths, now dust-covered, now water-logged; through your hidden corners and your open ranges; in August and in January. And you know the step of my horse. I have sought you everywhere, amongst the hardiest of oaks, in the most secluded of thickets, in the air and in clods of earth.

You are a river of beauty, moving, murmuring, adapting to the night, to the day, to the season. Over you I sense ancient steps, the same blood running in my veins. We are all like you, something which neither begins nor ends, like beauty or those rows of olive trees whose end my eyes never reach.

And we wait. At times it is a little harsh, this stirring of the heart. Everything on the outside is unchanging and something within is stirring. What will it be? A great wing-beat of love will draw us into its light. Everything will be cleansed. There in our little corner, love endures. Oh land! This beauty has neither page nor mirror, and only, sometimes, allows itself to be seduced by the trembling of words, by the suggestion of poetry. But to rein you in, to enclose you? Who puts gates on the land?

*'Poner puertas al campo' in Spanish, literally, 'to place gates on the land', a Spanish phrase about putting impossible restrictions on life, on nature.

LLEGAN LOS ABEJARUCOS

Hoy han venido los abejarucos y su llamada nos ha traído a la realidad de que la primavera va penetrando tremenda e imperiosa a pesar de los fríos retardados y de las últimas violetas, que se van como vinieron, inadvertidamente.

Ya están aquí los abejarucos. Andaba por la huerta y de pronto, una llamada leve que me hizo volver la cabeza al cielo. Insistió el silbido y me halle sin saber si era esta, si aquella primavera, si este, si aquel año. Un leve silbido había descompuesto el orden de día tras día, de horas y de fechas.

Y arriba, velocísimo, parado, fino, entre verde y amarillo, las alas y el pico agudos, con la primera abeja, el primer abejaruco. Cuando pasé por el colmenar había un rumor de pánico y una prisa por recogerse, inusitados en estas tardes en que hay ciruelos y membrillos en flor.

THE BEE-EATERS ARRIVE

The bee-eaters have arrived today, and their call has reminded us that spring is advancing, imperious and unstoppable, despite late cold spells and the last violets that are leaving as they came, unremarked.

Now the bee-eaters are here. I was walking through the orchard when suddenly a low call made me turn my head to the sky. The whistle was insistent, and I found myself not knowing if it was this spring or that spring, this year or that year. A light call had disrupted the sequence of days, of hours and dates.

And above, so fast, still, elegant – between green and yellow, with pointed beak and wings – the first bee-eater with the first bee. When I went by the hives there was a sound of panic, a rush to take refuge, unusual in these days of cherry trees and quinces in blossom.

PRIMERAS NOTICIAS

Sí, sí, son días de muchas noticias. No hay tiempo para verificarlas, ni para escribirlas, ni casi para gozarlas. Hay que ir de mata en mata, de zanja en vereda, de vallado en sendero, de sotillo en linde, para no perder tanta anunciación, tanto nacimiento, tanta esperanza. Y se nos va la mayor parte de la delicia sin recogerla. Acertamos, sí, a no perdernos el primer lirio, porque lo veníamos espiando a diario, siguiendo el tallo de mañana a tarde, hasta que al primer sol de hoy estaba tan natural y tan tranquilo, el primer lirio fuera. Lo notamos porque había un inusitado zumbar de abejas que lo sabían mejor que nosotros y que estaban alerta. ¡No habrá sido nada en la colmena cuando hayan llegado! ¡Qué de órdenes, qué prisa, qué gozo!

Poco a poco van viniendo todos. Hace unos días, las golondrinas al techo del comedor. Ayer, la primera flor de membrillo al par que la hoja. Ésta, de un vello suave y un verde lleno de tornasoles: aquélla, con un aroma que anuncia vagamente el otoño. El trigo se ensombrece y madura su verde cada día. La higuera y los perales comienzan a conmoverse. Y los granados y las yerbas.

EARLY SIGNS

Yes, truly, these days are full of things happening. There is no time to take them in, no time to write them down, hardly time to enjoy them. You have to go from bush to shrub, from ditch to track, from fence to footpath, from copse to field's edge, not to miss so many annunciations, so many births, so much hope. And the greater part of this delight passes us by without our savouring it. At least, yes, we make sure not to miss the first iris because we have been observing it day after day, noting the stem from morning till evening; until in the first sunshine of today, so natural, so tranquil, the first iris came out. We knew it because there was an unusual buzzing of bees who knew better than us and were ready. There would have been none remaining in the hive when the irises appeared! So many commands, such rushing about, such delight!

Little by little they are all arriving. A few days ago the swallows were on the ceiling of the dining-room; yesterday the first flower and the first leaf on the quince-tree, the leaf of soft down and a green of such iridescence, the flower with a scent vaguely suggesting autumn. The wheat is darkening, its green deeper day by day. The fig-trees and pear-trees begin to stir, and the pomegranates and the grasses.

SAZÓN DE TODO

Cada árbol tiene su sazón y su manera de madurar: los hay tímidos, los hay airosos, los hay torpes, como los animales y las personas; pero siempre en una relación dichosa con su forma y su tronco. Ahí tenéis a la higuera. Las ramas que peló el invierno, caen graciosamente curvadas de los troncos cenizosos. Apuntan como lanzas afiladas y, de pronto, unas hojas torpes que, al tercer día de aparecer y a distancia, se dirían de otro árbol (tal es el contraste entre su ternura y la dureza del tronco que las soporta), inesperadas, pendientes de la primera rama que salga en el aire a recibirlas. Los granados son otra cosa. Tanta dureza, tanta sequedad, para luego romper en este prodigio enrojecido, en este leve encendimiento, que pone las copas como ascuas fresquísimas, si cupiera el prodigio de un ascua fresquísima. ¿Y qué diremos de las encinas? ¿No habéis visto florecer una encina? No habéis visto nada de un temblor y nobleza semejante. Se enciende también levemente, pero no como el granado en ascua, sino en miel, en un dorado llover, que hace grande y tierno el aire alrededor. Ah si la flor de la encina oliera, ¿qué fuerza de olor no seria la suya, qué chorro de aroma colmando el campo todo? Y este manzano joven, aún sin hoja, que de pronto se ha puesto a dar flor y que parece un candelabro de flores, y que nos ha detenido hoy largo rato en nuestro paseo haciendo que nos preguntemos, cómo es posible tanta hermosura en tan poco lugar.

EVERYTHING HAS ITS SEASON

Each tree has its season and its way of maturing: some of them are shy, some gleeful, some clumsy, like animals and people; but always with a happy relation between shape and trunk. Here you have the fig-tree; its branches, stripped in winter, hang gracefully curved from the ash-grey trunk. They point like sharpened lances but soon a few limp leaves appear, attached to the first branch which rises into the air to receive them. By the third day and from a distance, you would say they belonged to a different tree, such is the contrast between their tenderness and the sturdiness of the trunk which supports them. The pomegranates are another thing. Such toughness, such dryness, and then to break out into that red, that light flame which makes its flowers seem like the freshest of glowing embers, if one could imagine the miracle of a fresh ember. And what shall we say about the holm oaks? Have you seen a holm oak come into flower? You have never seen such trembling, such nobility. It also ignites slowly but unlike the embers of the pomegranate, it is like honey, in a golden shower, that softens and expands the surrounding air. If the flower of the holm oak had its own aroma, how pungent it would be, how torrential the aroma flooding the entire countryside! And this young apple tree, still leafless, which has just blossomed and looks like a candelabra of flowers, and has arrested us for some while on our walk today, asking ourselves how there could be so much beauty in such a modest place.

LAS YERBAS IGNORADAS

¿Hasta cuándo voy a ignorar vuestros nombres? ¡Qué inesperadas, qué resueltas, qué sencillas, las yerbas ignoradas, qué huella el pie, que arranca el escardillo, que atropella el arado! Los que llaman nazarenos, la que dicen lechitrezna, los zapaticos del Niño Dios (que son el prodigio de finura con que Dios pisa la tierra), los jaramagos, y las mil plantas que llaman yerbas del campo, para borrarlas de una vez y que nos trae fielmente el viento de la primavera, a pesar de arado y escardillo. ¡Oh nobles yerbecillas!

El olor apenas se os advierte: sí la lozanía, sí el doblarse tremendo de vuestros tallos ante la reja fría, sí la dulzura con que reposáis sobre el surco abierto, sí vuestro triunfo sobre lindazos y veras donde no llega hierro alguno, y que convertís en caminos celestiales. ¡Oh, jaramagos, lenguazas, zapaticos, nazarenos, ignoradas yerbas del campo!

NEGLECTED GRASSES

How long am I going to remain ignorant of your names? Neglected grasses – so surprising, so resilient, so natural – trodden underfoot, uprooted by the hoe, flattened by the plough.

Those called Nazarenes, the ones they call Milkweed, and Slippers of the Christ Child (which have the miraculous lightness with which God walked on the earth), and Charlock, and a thousand plants called simply grasses of the field, to dismiss them once and for all, and yet which faithfully bring us the winds of spring, in spite of the plough and the hoe.

Oh, noble little grasses!

Your scent is hardly noticeable, but your vigour, the dramatic way you bend under the cold ploughshare, the sweet ease with which you rest upon the open furrow, and, yes, your triumph on steep banks and the edges of fields which no blade ever reaches and which you transform into heavenly paths. Oh, Charlock, Spurge, Little Slippers, Nazarenes, neglected grasses of the fields!

LAS HERRIZAS

Refugios de la hermosura, herrizas, únicos lugares donde la Naturaleza hace de las suyas bellísimas. Da gloria tras tanto campo arado, tras tanto olivo compuesto, tras tanto surco ordenado, tras tanto habar sin libertad, este puro reino de la libertad y la hermosura que son las herrizas. Gracias a que Dios puso piedras sobre las lomas y a las piedras solo Él las labra a fuerza de poder y florecen de hermosura. ¡Oh carrascas! ¡Oh acebuches! ¡Oh coscojas! ¡Oh torvisco, romerales, tomillos y lentiscos! ¡Oh toda mata áspera! ¡Oh silvestre libertad! Y donde menos se espera, en la rendija de dos piedras, en el minúsculo horadamiento de la roca, allí una tierra increíble donde crece el narciso silvestre, amarillo y aromoso, y el lirio blanco y azul, casi ángel de las flores.

Ya quedan pocas, pero ¡qué bien pagan estas herrizas la subida áspera, que recompensa la de las piedras generosas dando frutos de belleza! ¡Oh reino donde el arado no llega ni se hunde la planta del hombre! ¡Oh reino que bien puede compararse a la libertad!

STONY HILLSIDES

Refuges of beauty, stony hillsides, the only places nature makes so beautifully her own. Glorious, after so much ploughed land, so many ranks of olives, so many regular furrows, so many cramped acres of beans; these pure kingdoms of freedom and beauty which are the stone-covered hillsides. Thanks be to God for putting rocks on these slopes, and with rocks only He has the power to cultivate and bring forth such loveliness. Oh, shrub oaks, kermes oaks, wild olives! Mastic trees, wild daphne, rosemary and thyme! All the tough shrubs! Oh, the freedom of the wild! And where least expected, in the crack between two stones, in a tiny fissure of the rock, the miraculous soil where the wild daffodil grows, yellow and scented, and the white and blue iris, almost the angel of flowers.

Only a few remain now, yet how worthwhile the steep climb up those stony slopes, what a reward, the generous stones bringing forth such fruits of beauty. Oh, kingdom beyond the reach of the plough, where the foot of man cannot take hold! Oh, kingdom which can well be compared to freedom!

MIGUELILLO EL PAVERO

Es bajo, achaparradete, rubio, tostado, cabezón.
Yo le digo:
—Miguelillo, ¿cuántos años tienes?
—Catorce.
—¿Qué haces?
—No tengo nada que hacer.
—¿Y tus padres?
—No tengo.
—Pero hombre, Miguelillo.
Se queda un momento con la caña en suspenso.
—Miguelillo, ¿no tienes zapatos?
—No, señor.
—¡Pero hombre, Miguelillo
—Desde que se fue mi abuelo no tengo de nada. Antes, con los pájaros, se vivía. Los zorzales dan mucho. Mi abuelo ponía las perchas y yo iba a recogerlos. ¿Usted no ha visto los zorzales? En acabando la aceituna se van. A mí me extravían los zorzales todos los años cuando se van. Mientras hay zorzales se vive. Dos, tres docenas, según los días. Y ahora no tengo a nadie.
—¡Hombre!...
—Y hoy no he comido.
—¡Pero hombre, hombre, Miguelillo!

MIGUELILLO
WHO MINDS THE TURKEYS

He is short and stocky, fair-haired, sunburnt, headstrong.
I ask him:
'Miguelillo, how old are you?'
'Fourteen.'
'What do you do?'
'I have nothing to do'.
'And your parents?'
'I don't have any.'
'But surely, Miguelillo…'
He stops for a moment with his stick raised.
'Miguelillo, don't you have any shoes?'
'No, master.'
'But surely, Miguelillo!'
'Since my grandfather went away, I have nothing. Before, with the birds, I could get by. The thrushes provide a lot. My grandfather set the traps and I went out to collect them. Haven't you seen the thrushes? They leave when the olives are finished. I feel lost every year when the thrushes leave. While they are here, I can get by. Two, three dozen depending on the day. And now I have nobody.
'But how…'
'And today I have not eaten.'
'But how come, Miguelillo, how come?'

CUANDO FLORECEN LAS ENCINAS

Cuando florecen las encinas, decía, hay que temblar. Se anuda la delicia en la garganta. Pasa como cuando llora un hombre fuerte y maduro, cuando viene un estremecimiento a colmar una plenitud. Hay en ello algo humano, «sazón de todo». Igual con las encinas. Con las jóvenes y las viejas, que todas florecen. La hoja del chaparro es áspera, crujiente, graciosamente rizada en el contorno, verde el oscuro haz y gris el envés. El tronco áspero y duro se diría insensible. Se diría insensible el árbol entero, apenas conmovido por lluvia o viento, sol o hielo, un contemplativo, con mucho cilicio y poco halago. Y de pronto hay un estremecimiento y el árbol comienza a vestirse, y toda aquella dureza, aquella ascesis, se expresa en purísimo temblor, en goterones de ternura que la llenan toda, que la ponen como llovida de belleza, enmelada, soñadora, sauce sin río en el monte, con toda la fuerza de la encina y toda la melancolía del sauce.

Las encinas no se conocen a sí mismas cuando llega el florecimiento. Están tan enamoradas, que casi componen una figura patética en el paisaje, y teme uno que ni los pájaros ni los viandantes las tomen en serio y les suceda como a los gigantes enamorados que pierden el tino y el peso.

Luego, quisiera uno guardar el momento, conservar el temblor, detener el fruto y quedarse para siempre bajo tanta gracia y brío. Pero las noches de primavera suelen destemplarse y no se puede prolongar el crepúsculo bajo una encina florecida. Vendrá el relente y nos herirá la espalda y habremos de abandonar tanta hermosura a la noche.

WHEN THE HOLM OAKS FLOWER

They say when the holm oaks flower you should tremble. The sweetness constricts the throat. It is as if a strong and fully-grown man weeps, or when a tremor overwhelms plenitude. There is something human about it, a "ripeness of everything", the same as the holm oaks. Young or old, they all come into flower. The leaf of the oak is rough and brittle, its edges delicately curled, green on the dark side and grey on the other. The rough hard trunk you would say was without feeling. You would say the whole tree was without feeling, hardly affected by the wind and the rain, by sun or frost; a monk, all hair shirt and little gratification. Yet, all of a sudden, there is a slight quivering and the tree begins to clothe itself, and all that hardness, that asceticism, turns into the purest trembling, into little drops of tenderness which cover it completely, turning it into a cascade of beauty, honeyed, dream-like, a willow tree on a hill with no river, with all the strength of the oak and all the melancholy of the willow.

The holm oaks do not even recognise themselves when they blossom. They are so in love they cut an almost pathetic figure in the landscape; you worry neither birds nor passers-by will take them seriously. They become like love-struck giants, without gravity or moderation.

Afterwards, you want to hold onto the moment, preserve the tremor, delay the fruiting, and remain forever in the aura of so much ardour and grace. Spring nights, though, become cold and you cannot stay long under a flowering holm oak. Damp rises, you feel it in your back and have to abandon so much beauty to the night.

NARCISO EL CANTOR

¿Hasta cuándo, hasta cuándo vas a estar así, hijo, Narciso?
—Madre, ¡usted dirá! ¡Yo qué sé hasta cuándo voy a estar así!
—...Cantando como un tonto, siendo el baldón de la familia, la burla del pueblo? Ya ves todos los muchachos, uno sale, el otro entra, uno se aplica en la escuela, otro en el oficio y son la honra de la familia. Mira Gabrielillo qué letra tiene: dice el maestro que es un primor. Y José, el de la Romualda, se va a escardar con su padre todas las mañanas.
¡Y tú, Narciso, ahí sentado, canta que te canta, sin letra y sin oficio!
—Pero, madre, yo qué sé hasta cuándo voy a estar así. El maestro dice que no sirvo. Y padre con que salir a escardar no tengo. Madre, ¿qué hago si no canto?
—¡Hacer por hacer hay tantas cosas! Cepillar, cepillan los carpinteros, los panaderos amasan, los labradores aran, los herreros adoban el hierro.
—Madre, ¿y los cantores? ¿Qué hacen los cantores? ¿No cantan? ¿Por qué me puso Narciso, madre? Si yo me llamara José como el de la Romualda, o Florencio o Juanillo como los de la Antonia, yo sería labrador, pero imagínese, madre, a Narciso, su Narciso, con un escardillo o un martillo o un cepillo. Déjeme, madre, que si no me tengo que arrancar el nombre: Narciso, el Cantor. Y, ¿quién me va a conocer?

NARCISO THE SINGER

'How long, how long are you going to be like this, Narciso, my son?

'You tell me, Mother, I don't know how long I am going to be like this!

'...Singing like a crazy person, a disgrace to your family, the laughing-stock of the village. Look at all the other children, one leaves, another returns, one gets on in school, another has a trade, and they bring honour to their families. Look at little Gabriel, what handwriting he has, the schoolmaster says he's a star. And Romualda's son, José, every morning he goes to help his father with the hoeing.

'And you, Narciso, sitting there, singing, just singing, with no writing and no job!

'But Mother, I don't know how long I am going to be like this. The schoolmaster says I am no good and I don't have a father to go out and hoe with. What would I do if I didn't sing, Mother?

'Do! There are so many things to do! Plane wood! Carpenters plane wood, bakers knead, farm-workers plough, blacksmiths forge iron.

'And singers, Mother? What do singers do? Don't they sing? Why did you name me Narciso, Mother? If I was called José, like Romualda's son, or Florencio or Juanillo, like Antonia's children, I would be a farmworker; but imagine, Mother, Narciso, your Narciso, with a hoe or a hammer or a plane? Let me be, Mother, so I don't have to change my name: Narciso the Singer. And then, who is going to know me?'

LAS LILAS

¿De dónde vuestro olor que me va llenando, que me vacía de todo lo que no sea vuestra presencia, que me lleva al jardín aquel de las jupiteres, los bojes y los cipreses, el oratorio aquel que henchíais como un barco, por mares de delicia, rumbo al paraíso? ¿De dónde, adónde vuestro aroma?

Había un banco bajo el limonero. Ya estaban fuera las primeras rosas y recién ausentes las últimas violetas. Todavía el verdín del invierno hacia blandos los senderos, pero comenzábamos a buscar la delicia fría del chorro de la fuente. Y en cuanto se abrió la puerta del jardín y se bajaban los dos primeros escalones, ya estaba invisible, realísimo, el aroma de las lilas dándonos la bienvenida. Ya se andaba en otro mundo. Los ramos densos y morados o blancos, la hoja fina y lujuriosa, el olor como un cuerpo, la muerte dulce y aguardada, el seno y el cabello, el cobijo fresquísimo, el entresueño y la raíz de aquel mundo mejor, la huida, por fin, de todo a todo, a lomos de la dicha, dejando el cuerpo como una flor inútil que ya dio lo suyo.

LILACS

Where does your scent come from? This scent which is invading me, emptying me of everything except your presence, which takes me back to that garden, the one with the Jupiter shrubs, box hedges and cypresses, a chapel which you would fill so it became like a ship sailing to paradise through seas of delight. Where does your scent come from, where is it going?

There was a bench under the lemon tree. The first roses were out, and the last violets just finished. The lingering moss of winter made the paths soft underfoot, but we had begun to look forward to the delicious cold of the water gushing from the fountain. And when the garden gate was opened and we went down the first two steps, there it was, invisible, intensely real, the scent of the lilacs bidding us welcome. There we were entering another world. The dense stems purple or white, the leaf fine and luxuriant, the aroma like a body, death sweet and welcomed, tresses and soft flesh, the coolest refuge, the half-dream and origin of that better world; the flight, finally, from everything to everything, on the back of bliss, leaving the body like a useless flower now it has given up its essence.

LAS REJAS ENLUTADAS

Vamos a caballo por el campo recién mojado con las lluvias tardías de este mayo y está la tierra tan empapada, que cada casco al hundirse va dejando una huella que llena el agua. Los trigos, que ya tienen la cabeza pesada, comienzan a doblarse y hay muchas cebadas definitivamente vencidas. Aprovecha el sol la menor rajilla entre las nubes para colar una lanzada de luz y calor sobre los verdes que a el solo esperan para amarillear. Las zanjas rebosan flores en sus veras y se sueltan al aire los primeros insectos. La luz está fresca; un temblor lleno de gracia se cierne sobre los frutos que comienzan a cuajarse, sobre los olivos que tienen la flor a punto. Todo espera el clarinazo del calor. Es el paso delicado y gravísimo de la flor al fruto, cuando caen los pétalos de aquélla y se aprieta el primer indicio de éste, débil sobre la rama. Un puñalillo de frío mal venido en la madrugada, un sol apresurado, un viento traidor, y ese hilo que ata el fruto a la rama, se cortará y la savia no llegará a su termino. Todo el trabajo del año se vendrá a tierra por el momento despiadado. ¡Oh condición humana de la naturaleza! ¡Oh azar!

Vamos a caballo y oigo tras de mí:

—Como está la tierra tan pegajosa se enlutan las rejas y no se puede arar.

«Se enlutan las puntas de las rejas, se enlutan las puntas de las rejas», me quedo yo pensando maravillado de la justeza de la expresión en estos labios, mientras entramos en el sembrado y las espigas barren ásperas y amorosas los ijares de nuestros caballos.

PLOUGHSHARES IN MOURNING

We are riding across fields still wet after the late rains in this month of May and the ground is so sodden that as each hoof sinks in it leaves an imprint that fills with water. The standing wheat, already heavy-headed, is beginning to double over and much of the barley is fully ripe. The sun takes advantage of the slightest break in the clouds to send down a shaft of light and warmth onto greens only awaiting full sun to become yellow. Wildflowers are abundant on the banks of ditches and the first insects are in the air. The light is fresh; a trembling full of grace is hovering over the fruit trees which are starting to bud, and over the olive trees, with their flowers just appearing. Everything awaits the clarion call of heat. It is that delicate and critical step from the flower to the fruit, when the petals fall from the former and leave the first sign of the latter, fragile on the branch. A little stab of cold air arriving unexpectedly in the early morning, a burst of early sun, a treacherous wind, and that thread which attaches the fruit to the branch would be severed and the sap never reach its goal. The whole year's work cast down on the ground in that cruel moment. Oh, the human condition of nature! Oh, ill fortune!

We are riding and behind me I hear:

'How muddy the ground is, the ploughshares will be in mourning and we won't be able to till the field'.

'The ploughshares will be in mourning, the ploughshares will be in mourning', it left me thinking, marvelling at the rightness of the expression on those lips, as we enter the sown fields, the spears of wheat brushing drily and lovingly against the flanks of our horses.

LAS AMAZONAS

Los caballejos valían poco. Un caballejo y una yegüecilla. Más bien hambrientos, más bien huesudos. Los atajarres valían poco: sillas inglesas, bocados y cabezadas andaluces. Las que valían eran ellas. Y eso que estaban viejas. Ana María iba por los sesenta y tantos. Josefa, por los sesenta. Una nació el día de San Marcos, la otra el de San Matías. Destino de hombres, como ellas decían. Hasta teníamos los nombres puestos. Alguien torció la cosa y salieron hembras. Por eso debajo de la falda usaban pantalones y el pelo se lo atusaban porque no se atrevían a cortárselo del todo.

Y donde ponían el ojo, ponían la bala, fuera lo que fuera, perdiz o aguilucho, corazón o fruto...

Solían andar de noche y siempre a caballo; elegían trochas y atajos, lindazos y veredas, caminos polvorientos entre olivares, caminos encharcados donde los caballos se hundían hasta los corvejones. Siempre juntas, siempre solas, siempre a lo mismo, siempre armadas, misteriosamente, nadie sabia adonde. Si a algún viandante, fuera de horas, le sucedía hallárselas, torcía el rumbo, o se agazapaba tras un tronco o sobre la tierra. Supersticiosamente las huían. Hablaban poco. Nadie las oyó cantar nunca; pero mantenían en el cortijo a uno, Periquillo el de Atrás, para que les cantara cuando quisieran.

Decían que Periquillo tenia voz de ángel y oyéndolo, es cuando a ellas se las vio más cerca de algo parecido a la lagrima.

Sus enemigos eran los recaudadores de arbitrios y contribuciones.

—En sesenta y tantos años de vida, no hemos pagado uno. Ni nuestro difundo padre, que en gloria éste.

Creían que el Estado era mentira, que lo inventaban unos cuantos sinvergüenzas para sacarle el dinero a los infelices.

AMAZONS

Their mounts were poor. A pony and a filly, rather hungry, rather bony. Their riding gear of little worth: English saddles, Andalusian bridles and bits. It was they who were worthy of note. Even old as they were, Ana María in her late sixties or more, Josefa still in her sixties. One born on Saint Mark's day, the other on Saint Matthew's. Destined to be men, as they said, we were even given names. But someone turned things around and they emerged as women. That was why they wore trousers under their skirts and cropped their hair which they didn't dare to cut completely.

Where their eye alighted, their aim was true, whatever it was, partridge or eaglet, heart or fruit.

They used to go out at night, always on horseback; keeping to shortcuts and byways, field edges and tracks, dusty paths through the olive fields, flooded lanes where their horses sank up to their fetlocks. Always together, always alone, always the same, always armed, secretively, nobody knew where they went. If some late traveller came across them, he would quicken his pace or crouch behind a tree or on the ground. Superstitiously they were avoided. They seldom spoke. Nobody ever heard them sing; but in the farmhouse they kept someone, Periquillo from Atrás, so that he could sing to them whenever they wanted.

It was said that Periquillo had the voice of an angel and listening to him was when they seemed closest to tears.

Their enemies were the collectors of tithes and taxes.

'In sixty and more years of life we have never paid once and neither did our departed father, may he rest in peace.'

They thought the State was a lie invented by some scoundrels to extract money from the less fortunate.

—No a nosotras, mientras montemos.

Fueron inútiles amenazas, anuncios en todos los boletines, apremios. Cuando la cosa se puso seria y apareció la Guardia Civil, desaparecieron ellas. Un mes pasaron por esos olivares, rondando de noche el cortijo, durmiendo donde les cogía, comiendo a horcajadas, esperando que se fuera la fuerza, que cuando la fuerza se fuera ya se entenderían ellas con los nuevos ocupantes, si es que alguien se atrevía. A tiro limpio, no de otra manera. Dos sombras por los olivares, furtivas, singulares, parte de la tierra misma.

'Not from us, not as long as we can ride.'

Threats, rewards, debt demands, announcements in all official bulletins, were useless. When the situation became serious and the Guardia Civil arrived, they disappeared. They spent a month in those olive fields, circling the farm at night, sleeping wherever night found them, eating in the saddle, waiting for the forces of law and order to leave; for when the forces went away they would reach an understanding with the new tenants, if anyone had dared. A clean shot if no other way. Two shadows in the olive fields, furtive, singular, part of the earth itself.

LAS NUBES

¿De dónde, ligeras, pesadas, blancas, grises, pasajeras del cielo, amantes del viento, vosotras nubes? ¿Qué sería de los cielos sin vosotras a quienes desgarran las montañas y a quienes tan dulcemente se entregan lomas y cerros? Cuando va vuestra sombra sobre los llanos, cuando se pliega sobre los barrancos, cuando parte en claros y oscuros los trigos, cuando bajáis tremendas, o graciosas subís, subís, vosotras nubes, nostalgia de la tierra, ligeras desterradas, apresuradas amantes, cuyo besar nunca es largo, cuyo destino es tan humano que está pendiente del primer viento.

—Ya están ahí las nubes, dicen los labradores. Y vuestra enorme presencia muda, llenando el cielo, añade no sé qué misterio a la vida. Ya están ahí las nubes.

Es un ligero humo blanco primero, tenue, casi invisible, un algodoncillo sobre la sierra que se confunde con la nieve, y luego unas manos inmensas que van palpando el azul, estrujándolo, ciñéndole, abriéndolo en grandes lagunas por donde se escapan los ojos.

—Ya están ahí las nubes.

Y las nubes, como los enamorados, se hacen huidizas con el deseo e impertinentes con la abundancia. Pero su presencia llena como su nombre, como su fecundidad.

CLOUDS

Clouds – light, dense, white, grey, travellers in the heavens, lovers of the wind – clouds, where are you coming from? What would the skies be without you; you who are torn by mountains and to whom hillsides and ridges surrender themselves so gently? When your shadow passes over the plain, when it bends into ravines, when it divides the fields of wheat into dark and light, when you are low and threatening or rise graciously up, and up; you, clouds, with your nostalgia for the land; weightless exiles, hurrying lovers, whose kiss never lingers, whose destiny is so human that it hangs upon the first wind.

'The clouds are here now', say the workers in the field. And your huge, silent presence, filling the sky, adds unknowable mystery to life, 'The clouds are here now.'

At first a light puff of smoke, faint, hardly visible, a fluff of cotton on the sierra that could be taken for snow, and then huge hands that are touching the blue, squeezing it, clinging to it, opening it into great pools through which the eye escapes.

'The clouds are here now.'

And the clouds, like lovers, become timid with desire and impudent with excess. But their presence is pervasive, like their name, like their fecundity.

II

II

LAS GAYOMBAS

Ya están despuntando las primeras gayombas. No puedo verlas sin estremecerme. Y menos olerlas. ¡Qué agolparse de tiempos, de personas, de ocasiones los que empuja esta flor amarilla, este meloso olor dentro del alma!

—¡Ya han llegado las gayombas! ¡Ya han llegado las gayombas!

Llenaban la casa de amarillo, ponían el aire hecho una cañada de hermosura con su olor, convertían las habitaciones cerradas al primer calor intempestivo en nidos oscuros de delicia y aroma donde podía uno quedarse horas y horas adivinando el palidecer del sol en las rajillas que dejaban los postigos entornados. Se podía cabalgar materialmente en aquel largo y redondo caballo del olor de las gayombas por tantos mundos entrevistos y deseados, por tantos hombros en los que apenas nos atrevíamos a poner el pensamiento, se podía partiendo de él llegar a tantas partes, que aguardábamos la llegada triunfal de las gayombas en el serón del borrico de la Alhalajuela, como el mejor regalo del mundo.

¡Oh hermosura! La flor tiene mucho de mariposa puramente amarilla parada en el junco fino y acerado de la planta. Son miles de amarillas mariposas paradas, oliendo, encendiendo el aire, alegrando las cañadas y los barrancos, las veras de los caminos.

YELLOW BROOM

The first broom is appearing. I never see it without excitement, and even more so when I catch its scent. What a hoard of past times, of people and events, arrive with this yellow flower, this honeyed scent within my soul!

'The broom's here now! The broom's here now!'

The house was filled with yellow, the air became a channel of beauty with its fragrance, rooms closed at the first unseasonal sign of heat became dark lairs of rapture and aroma in which one could pass hour upon hour observing the sun turning pale on the little bars created by half-open shutters. You could really ride on that long and voluminous steed of the broom's scent; to so many worlds, dimly perceived and desired; upon so many shoulders* on which we scarcely dared let our thoughts dwell. You could reach so many places, starting here, with the triumphant arrival of the broom in the baskets of the donkey from Alhalajuela, the finest gift in all the world.

Oh, beauty! The flower has much of the pure yellow of a butterfly resting on the sharp and slender stem of a plant; thousands of motionless yellow butterflies, scenting, lighting up the air, bringing joy to ravines and gullies and the borders of paths.

---

* 'hombres' (men) in earlier editions, 'hombros' (shoulders) in the 1999 edition.

LOS JARAMAGOS

El año está siendo de jaramagos. ¿Qué ángeles amarillos, de dónde han venido, cuando que no los vimos, a sembrar jaramagos y más jaramagos en el campo? Parece como si un inmenso pintor con una brocha anchísima se hubiera entretenido en ir pintando de amarillo las camadas de los olivos, punteando de amarillo zanjas y lindes, cercados y senderos, dejando en claro los redondeles de los olivos, los sembrados que limpió el escardillo. El campo es una gran sinfonía en amarillo donde apenas dan una leve nota, blancos de nievecillas, morados de lenguazas y nazarenos, rojos de amapolas y aquellas florecillas, que el jaramagal, que llega ya a la cruz de los olivos y a los ijares de los caballos, permite florecer. ¡Qué fuerza de fecundidad, qué propaganda para los vientos o ángeles que traen en sus faldas las semillas, qué rabia de los arados, con las inútiles rejas enlutadas, frente a esta victoria del jaramago que quiere volver el mundo a la libertad!

Y van las riadas amarillas por las camadas, inmensas, reposadas, incansables, bellísimas, y en los cercados son mares amarillas, y en las lindes, hilos, y dondequiera grito tremendo de la naturaleza por sus fueros. Y donde llega a alcanzarlos la reja, cuerpo mortecino y doblado, hacinamiento inútil, ejemplo de loca gallardía.

—Nunca se han visto tantos jaramagales como este año, dicen las gentes.

CHARLOCK

This is becoming the year of charlock. Those yellow angels, where have they come from, when we didn't see them, sowing more and more charlock in the fields? It's as if an immense painter with the broadest of brushes had undertaken to paint the fields of olives yellow, highlighting with yellow the ditches and borders, paths and meadows, leaving the areas around the trees bare, the ground cleared by the hoe. The land is a great symphony of yellow in which there are hardly any lighter notes, whites of snowdrops, purples of hound's tongue and grape hyacinth, reds of poppies and those little flowers the charlock allows to grow amongst stalks already as high as the branching of the olives and the flanks of the horses. What force of fertility, what propaganda for the winds or angels carrying the seeds in their garments, what rage for the ploughs, their blades useless, in mourning, before this victory of charlock wishing to return the world to freedom!

And floods of yellow run along the lines of olives, immense, unhurried, untiring, so beautiful; and in the meadows, seas of yellow, and threads at the field borders, and everywhere, a great cry of nature claiming its rights. And where the blade of the plough reaches them, lifeless bodies doubled over, heaped uselessly, an example of crazy gallantry.

'There's never been as much charlock as this year', country people are saying.

LAS TÓRTOLAS

Están recién llegadas. Ya empiezan a atar olivo a olivo, con susurro y con vuelo, con abaniquillos blancos que se abren y los van zurciendo. Yo no sé por qué el zureo de la tórtola abre en el campo al alma unos tan largos túneles de ternura, unas penumbras tan frescas al oído. El alma se acompasa a esta monotonía y siente el aire entero vibrar como un mar cuyas olas dan en sus orillas, acordadas al lento envió del sonido.

Cuando la tórtola llega, comienza a negrear la espiga. ¿Qué sería de este aire de estío sin ese alivio y acompasamiento de las tórtolas? Ellas saben el camino de la fuente, la gallardía de la figura, la delicadeza en el vuelo, el ajuste del rumor. Encienden el campo, enternecen los olivos, suavizan el terrón reseco del agosto, la dureza de los rastrojos. Llevan la paz en los ojos y su cuello se comporta tan ajustadamente a las reglas de la gracia, se contrae, se yergue, se revuelve, que ni siquiera es disculpa para aprisionarlas. ¡Oh tórtolas del verano y el olivar!

TURTLE DOVES

They have just arrived. Already they are beginning to thread olive tree to olive tree, with soft call and flight, with white fantails that open as they stitch on and on. I don't know why the cooing of a dove in the fields opens the soul to such long tunnels of tenderness, to shadows so fresh to the ear. The soul adapts to this single note and feels the air all around vibrate like the waves of the sea reaching the shore, in step with the slow release of the sound.

When the turtle dove appears, the ears of wheat start to darken. What would the air of summer be like without this relief, this accompaniment of doves? They know the path to the spring, the body's poise, delicacy of flight, modulation of call. They light up the land, make the olive trees tender, soften the hard dry earth of August, the brittleness of the stubble. They bring peace in their eyes, and their necks move in such accord with the rules of gracefulness, holding back, straightening up, turning around. But that is no excuse for imprisoning them. Oh, turtle doves of summer and the olive fields!

JUANILLO

Juanillo el loco, capitán general de estos ejércitos de olivos, a quienes habla como soldados cuando sopla el solano y lo trastorna.
¿De dónde sale Juanillo? Nadie lo sabe. Aparece, sí, a las horas de comer. Ni le importa el calor, ni el frío, ni el dormir, ni el vestido: le importa comer. Ni el dinero: si acaso afeitarse. Ni andar descalzo.
—Ya ve usted, un pedacillo de pan es todo lo que comí esta madrugada.
Y comerá devoradoramente lo que le ofrezcáis. Y se ira luego al campo, sin dirección, hablando solo, dirigiéndose a quien tenga cerca, árbol o roca, terrón o nube, planteándoles sus problemas que no dejan de ser espeluznantes.
Yo, ¿para qué estoy aquí? ¿Para nada? Andar, andar, para qué? Ahí puedes seguir sol apretando, achicharrando, que ya te cansarás: ¡Olivos! ¡Atención! ¡En marcha!
Y así le van las horas. No duerme. Come y come. Anda y come. Habla de una hermana suya. Dice que está lejos, que él no la conoce, que es su hermana, que vendrá. Está seguro que tiene una hermana, todos tenemos una hermana. Vendrá siempre.
—Juanillo, ¿quieres unos zapatos?
—Ya ves tu, ¿no voy a querer unos zapatos?
Le doy unos zapatos y se va. Cuando llega al olivar se los quita. Los cuelga de una rama. Cuando vuelve se los pone otra vez y entra pisando fuerte, por el patio, derecho a la cocina.
—Juanillo, ¿no tienes novia?
—¿Novia? Ya ves tú, ¿no voy a tener novia? Tengo novia pero no lo digo.

JUANILLO

Crazy Juanillo, commander in chief of these armies of olive trees he addresses as if they were soldiers when the solano* blows and turns his mind.

Where does Juanillo come from? No one knows. He appears, though, when it's time to eat. He doesn't care about heat or cold or how he is dressed or about sleeping. He cares about eating. And he doesn't care about money, but, perhaps, yes, to have a shave. Nor about going barefoot.

'You see, all I ate at dawn was a crust of bread.'

But he'll eat greedily what he's offered. Then he goes off to the fields, to nowhere in particular, talking to himself, or to whatever is close, tree or rock, clod or cloud, explaining his problems which are always hair-raising.

"Me? What am I doing here? For nothing. Going on and on … and what for? You, Sun, you can carry on, beating down on me, burning me, but you'll get tired. Olives, to attention! Quick march!

And so, the hours go by. He doesn't sleep. He eats and eats. He marches and eats. He talks about a sister of his. He says that she lives far away, that he doesn't know her, that she's his sister, she will come. He's sure he has a sister, all of us have a sister. She'll always come back.

'Juanillo, do you want a pair of shoes?'

'What a question! How could I not want shoes!'

I gave him the shoes and off he goes. When he gets to the olive fields, he takes them off. He hangs them on a branch. When he returns, he puts them on again and comes in through the patio with a heavy step, heading to the kitchen.

'Juanillo, don't you have a girlfriend?

'A girlfriend? Oof, why wouldn't I have a girlfriend? I have a girlfriend, but I don't talk about it.'

—Y, ¿cuándo te casas?

—Digo, ¡cuándo me caso! ¡Como si hiciera falta casarse para tener novia! Tengo novia. En cuanto estoy solo se me pega. Por eso no la veis, porque no se me pega más que cuando estoy solo. No se la ve más que en los olivares.

En invierno, Juanillo pone perchas para los zorzales y las revisa a diario. De sus bolsillos inflados comienzan a salir zorzales y más zorzales, la pluma bellísima, los cuellos lacios, el pico inerte.

Y cuando no hay zorzales, Juanillo coge su hacha y se va al enemigo: cualquier troncón durísimo de olivo al que increpa y destroza. Cuando acaba, sonríe y retorna:

—Ya está muerto. Éste no resucita.

'And when are you getting married?

'Oof! You ask me when I am getting married! As if you have to marry to have girlfriend! I have a girlfriend. She comes close to me when I am alone. That's why you don't see her, she only comes close to me when I am alone. You'll only see her amongst the olives.

In winter, Juanillo puts out traps for the thrushes and checks them every day. The birds begin to stick out of his bulging pockets, more and more thrushes, with their beautiful feathers, their necks limp and their beaks useless.

And when there are no thrushes, Juanillo takes his axe and goes after the enemy: any of the toughest boughs of the olive trees, which he rebukes and destroys. When he's finished, he smiles and comes back.

'It's dead now. This one won't come back to life.'

*El solano, a late summer wind in the region of Antequera

LOS ÁLAMOS BLANCOS

Alegría de los álamos blancos era el verano! Alegría de envés de plata y haz de verde, juego en el viento y en la luz, marecilla de frescor en la calina, ligereza al peso que el verano echa sobre los días. Alivia el mediodía contemplarlos, toma la hora ingrávida y por la noche, con la luna, hacen volver las viejas fábulas. El álamo blanco halla su luz, la luz lunar su mejor oficio. Entonces, sí que el tembleteo, el rumor, la caricia, se hacen vívidos, humanos casi. Allí halla la tórtola su habitación mejor y abajo el lagarto, entre la maleza, su casa.

¡Ay, lástima de amantes para estos lechos, de cifras para estas cortezas!

WHITE POPLARS

Summertime was the joy of white poplars! The joy of their leaves, one side silver the other green, playing in the light and in the wind, a little sea of freshness in the haze, lightening the pall summer casts over the days. What a sweet relief to contemplate them at midday, scarcely aware of the hour; and at night, under the moon, when they bring old tales to mind. Then the white poplar finds its own light, the light of the moon, its best moment. And the quivering, rustling, caressing brings them to life, almost human. There the turtle dove finds its perfect habitat and, down below, the lizard its home in the undergrowth.

How sad there are no lovers for those beds, or dates on the bark!

EL VERANO

Pasó el reinado del jaramago. Pasó la trama en los olivos. Reinan los nerdos; el sembrado es rastrojo. Comienzan a perderse las codornices. El zureo de las tórtolas es menos fresco. Las zarzamoras deslíen su florecilla malva en el vallado y la matalahúga pierde a diario plata de su cabeza. El viento es seco y duro. Las aceitunas engordan. Los caminos son polvorientos. Apenas si a la luz primera o la brisa última del atardecer, los hacen transitables. Polvo y dureza en el campo. Reina lo duro: el olivo, la paja reseca. El verde se defiende mal. Al centro del día el campo se queda mudo. Tal vez la chicharra. Que no se sienta un arroyo que el campo entero se volcara de sed. Tanta tiene. Hay que dejar que el sol se desfogue y buscar la sombra, la recachita, la penumbra en las bodegas húmedas, las cuadras silenciosas. Hasta la luz de la luna parece tibia como el agua de la alberca o las piedras que el sol calentó todo el día. Pero la era sigue su rueda al trote cansino de las yeguas. Crujen los trillos, salta la gavilla, dormitan los gañanes. Al primer anuncio de brisa, ya están aventando. El *biergo* y el viento hacen cada uno lo suyo y el grano cae. Luego henchirá los trojes, se repartirá, tornará a caer en el surco, será briznilla, caña juncal, hoja ancha. Será espiga y pasto de era.

Con un filo de luna en el cielo nos volvemos. Los maíces tienen un peculiar rumor con el viento: suenan a acero. Y por el camino, entre el polvo, brillan y desaparecen, conforme vamos avanzando, los ojos encendidos de las zumayas.

SUMMER

The reign of charlock has ended, the olive trees have flowered, corn parsley is taking over, sown fields are stubble now. Quails have become difficult to spot, the cooing of the turtle dove begins to weary. The blackberries are opening their pale little purple flowers on the hedges and the heads of anise plants are losing their silver day by day. The wind is dry and fierce. The olives are swelling. Dust covers paths usable only at first light or in the last breath of wind in the evening. The fields are dusty and unyielding. Hardy things reign, the olives trees, the brittle straw. Green has few defences. The fields are mute at midday, except for the cicadas. If it sensed a stream the whole land would erupt with thirst. It is so parched. You have to allow the sun to exhaust itself and look for shade, a little shelter, the half-light in damp cellars, the silent stables. Even the light of the moon seems tepid, like the water in the cistern or the stones the sun has warmed throughout the day. But on the threshing floor the mares circle with their weary tread. The threshing boards creak, the sheaves are jumping, the farmhands doze. At the first sign of wind the winnowing begins. The breeze and the forks do their work and the grain falls. Afterwards it will fill the granaries, and be distributed, sown again in the furrows, becoming little blades, stalks, wide leaves. It will become ears of corn and fodder for animals.

We are returning with a sliver of moon in the sky. The wind in the corn makes a strange sound, the sound of metal. And on our path, in the dust, the bright eyes of the owls shine and fade as we pass.

LA BARCINA

El calor es tremendo. Llega a todas partes. No perdona lugar ni ocasión. Tiene las horas empapadas. Azota el campo. Va el verano tumbando las gavillas, dándole una doliente belleza al sembrado erguido, señalando su huella con un poco de sequedad más, venciendo un poco más la madurez. Los pegujales que quedan en pie, humillan la espiga y piden la hoz para el descanso sobre la tierra que ya no les puede dar nada. Vienen los barcinadores y van cargando las gavillas en el carro.

De madrugada, que es la hora de la barcina, cuando carean los ganados. Se siente el mordisqueo de los mulos, el cencerro perdido. Se anuncia el día, quebrando el cielo un filillo lívido. El calor sigue posado, inmenso sobre la tierra.

Cuando amanezca, correrá un airecillo sin espigas que acariciar. Mañana el granero se henchirá otro poco y la tierra se ofrecerá desnuda al sol para que la purifique.

HARVESTING

The heat is tremendous. It gets everywhere. It spares no time and no place. Hours pass bathed in sweat. It beats down on the fields. Summer advancing and the shocks falling, lending an aching beauty to the uncut crop, leaving its trace, a little more aridity, ripeness further vanquished. In the fields where wheat is still standing, the ears are bent over, pleading for the sickle to rest on ground that can give them nothing more. The harvesters arrive and begin loading the shocks onto their wagons.

Dawn is the hour for bringing in the wheat, when the animals are grazing. You hear the mules chomping, somewhere the sound of bells. Day is announced, tearing the heavens with a livid thread. The heat is still there, settled, immense over the land.

With the dawn comes a breath of air running free, without wheat ears to caress. Tomorrow the barns will be a little fuller and the earth will offer itself naked under the purifying sun.

LOS INSTRUMENTOS
DEL VERANO

¡Que bellos, estos instrumentos del verano! Las horcas, las palas, los *biergos,* las carretas con sus varales. Cuando llega la feria de mayo, se reponen. Vienen ya lisos, pero más lisos los pondrán espigas, raspas y manos. Correrán por la palma suavemente, serán alas levantando la parva, lucirán desnudos al sol. Vienen los carros bamboleantes, más altos que los olivos, cortando pesadamente el duro verdor de éstos con su pajizo pasado, suspendiendo a su paso el zurear de las tórtolas, levantando las alondras cantoras.

Gusto imaginarme al dios del verano, coronado de espigas, cercado de estos instrumentos. Las tardes se alargan por el cielo y entregan el campo crujiente a la noche. El grillo recibe el canto de la cigarra y nunca se interrumpe el hilo de la continuada armonía. Vamos por el rastrojo y cruje. La sierra se aviolenta y con el sol último incendia su perfil. Las cosas van recobrando su contorno a esta luz que no ciega. Ahora se puede salir al campo, tumbarse en la era, encararse con las estrellas, escuchar el corazón del mundo. Ahora suena el agua en la reguera, la copla en la realenga, los pasos de las bestias en el careo.

El insecto entra en su reino. Inesperadamente, en los alamillos del soto, un pájaro. Silencio. Silencio que se hace grande, sobre el campo. Y Dios está arriba rodando, haciendo su música. Vamos viviendo.

THE IMPLEMENTS
OF SUMMER

How beautiful, these implements of summer! The hayforks, winnowing forks and spades, the wagons with their wooden shafts. They are brought out once more for the May Fair. Already smooth to the touch, but made smoother still by hands, by the husks and spears of corn. They slide easily in the palm, they will become wings raising the chaff, shining naked in the sun. The wagons come trundling, taller than the olives, the straw-colour of the hay cutting across the olives' austere green, silencing in passing the song of the turtle doves, causing the singing larks to ascend.

I like to imagine the god of summer crowned with spears of corn and surrounded by these implements. Evenings lengthen under the sky and bring night to the crackling fields. The cricket hears the song of the cicada and nothing interrupts the thread of continuous harmony. There is a rustling as we go through the stubble. The sierra becomes violet, the last sun is lighting its edges. Things recover their outline in this light which is not blinding. Now you can go out into the fields, lie down on the threshing floor, look up at the stars, listen to the heartbeat of the world. Now the sound of water in irrigation channels, snatches of song from the paths, the movement of animals in the pasture.

The insect comes into its kingdom. Unexpectedly, a bird appears amongst the young poplars by the river. Silence. Silence that becomes vast over the fields. And God is above, surrounding us, making His music. We live on…

EL VELADOR

Del pensador al velador va lo que va del invierno al verano, de largas noches en la cuadra a cortas noches al raso, bajo las estrellas.
—Lo mismo da, dice José. En invierno lo bueno es el calorcito de la cuadra. En verano, el fresquito de la noche en el campo. La cuestión, velador o pensador, es no dormir, si se quiere que el ganado éste bueno y no le cojan a uno traspuesto, por bien que venga en agosto, un sueño al frescor de la noche, bajo las estrellas o la luna, el perro al lado, no se presente cualquier cuatrero a pegárnosla.

Al volver los mulos de la besana ya esta José esperándolos, las martaguillas y las trabas dispuestas, los cencerros preparados, la manta terciada: el relente de la madrugada la pide. Los mulos lo conocen y entregan sus cabezas, se alinean y José monta a mujeriegas en el más viejo. Saben que los llevara donde abunde la espiga olvidada, donde el maojo esté más tierno. Los trabará al llegar y ellos se revolcarán para limpiarse del calor y el polvo del día. Luego, cencerros y dientes, compondrán un rumor acompasado al de los grillos, cárabos y bestezuelas nocturnas que aprovecharan la noche para ir tras la presa descuidada. José se arrebuja en un lindazo sobre su manta y deja que las estrellas rueden hondas en el cielo y los mulos careen —monstruosas sombras— en la oscuridad, que sólo algún rastrojo ardiendo rompe con su filo de fuego.

NIGHT GUARDIAN

From feeder to watcher is the same as from winter to summer, from long nights in the stables to short nights in the open under the stars.

'It's the same', says José, 'the good thing about winter is the warmth of the stable. In summer, the coolness of nights in the fields. The important thing, stable or field, is not to sleep, for the good of the animals, not to be caught dozing, good as it would be when August comes to sleep in the freshness of the night under the stars or the moon, a dog at one's side. It is then that a horse thief might strike.'

When the mules return from tilling the fields, José is there waiting for them, with fetters and harness ready, their cowbells sorted, the folded blanket he will need for the morning dew. The animals know him and turn to him; they line up and he mounts the oldest side-saddle. They know he will take them to where wheat is still abundant, where the corn husks are sweetest. On arriving he will hobble them, and they will lie down and roll over to clean themselves after the heat and dust of the day. Then, bells and chomping will become a chorus accompanying the sound of crickets and owls and the little night creatures which take advantage of the dark to stalk their unwary prey. José wraps himself in his blanket at the side of the field, leaving the stars to turn deep in the firmament and the mules to graze – monstrous shadows – in darkness broken only by some late burning stubble with its thread of fire.

LOS MELONARES

Este año los melones están regulares. Vinieron mal las aguas y se los llevaron en parte las tormentas. Hubieron de resembrarse y llegan apresurados y tarde. Otros años, por este tiempo, ya habían desarrollado las hojas tremendas, abierto las flores grandes y breves, lanzado las rastras. Este año, llevan un mes de retraso. Veremos cómo paran. Ninguna planta como el melón para buscar la humedad última de la tierra, para el apresurado trabajo de sacarle lo suyo y convertirlo en jugo de frescor y azúcar, en refrigerio de la siesta. Son las únicas isletas de frescura en este mar caliginoso del verano.

En la chocilla los niños del melonero esperan impacientes el primer fruto, como un regalo de la tierra. Van desmenuzando terrones, arrancando la grama tenaz, alisando las calles entre las matas. Espían hoja a hoja, el fruto esperado. Y el primer melón, los pondrá perdidos de churretes, goteantes las manos de azúcar liquida, brillantes los ojos.

Los ojos del padre espían otra cosa. Dice:

—Veremos a ver si los melones estos nos visten o no nos visten.

THE MELON BEDS

This year the melons are average. The rains came at the wrong time and the storms washed part of the crop away. They had to be seeded again and they are growing late and too quickly. In other years, by this time, the huge leaves had already appeared, their large short-lived flowers open and their runners extended. This year they are a month late. We'll see how they fare. There is no plant like the melon for finding the last moisture in the ground, for the urgent task of absorbing it and turning it into juice of such freshness and sweetness, into a treat for the siesta. These are the only little islands of freshness in the hazy sea of summer.

In the hut the children of the melon-grower wait impatiently for the first fruit, as a gift from the earth. They are breaking up the clods of soil, pulling out stubborn weeds, treading down the channels between the beds. They are spying, leaf by leaf, for the expected fruit. And the first melon finds them with sticky faces, hands dripping with the liquid sugar, and eyes shining.

The eyes of their father are looking for something else. He says:

'Let's see if these melons are going to put clothes on our backs, or not…'

EL SOLANO

¡Qué de noches, qué de tardes, qué de desolaciones tiene en su haber el solano!
—Ya está ahí el solano.
Se anuncia con un estremecimiento del aire, que apenas es nada y es el comienzo del solano. Se siente en los arboles, en los pájaros, en los dedos.
—Ya está ahí el solano.
Y puntualmente, comenzando en brisa fría o caliente para acabar en huracán, apresurando nubarrones sobre la sierra, destemplándolo todo, el solano. Es un viento con cuerpo.
Cuando sacude las puertas, cuando tuerce las esquinas, cuando afila las torres, cuando emboca los barrancos o se extiende por la vega, se sienten sus manos enormes, su pecho tremendo. Un cuerpo que por la noche se hace oscuro, que conoce todos los miedos para los niños, el rumor peor, el atajo al pavor.
—Ya está ahí el solano.
Tiembla la espiga y la aceituna, el nido y la azucena, el hombre y la cabaña. Lo traen San Juan, la Virgen del Carmen, la de Agosto. Y nunca trae pan, nunca vino, nunca aceite. Pero, ¡cuántas de estas florecillas y estos árboles no le deberán la fecundidad! El solano, sólo tiene voz para sus malas hazañas, la que enhuera la espiga y merma la aceituna.

THE SOLANO

How many days, how many nights, how much anguish comes with the solano!

'The solano's here.'

It is preceded by a trembling in the air, which is almost nothing but is the beginning of the solano. You sense it in the trees, in the birds, in your fingers.

'The solano's here.'

And, promptly, starting with a gust of hot or cold air and ending with a windstorm, pushing dark clouds over the sierras, upsetting everything, the solano. This is a wind with body.

When it shakes doors, when it whips round corners, when it scrapes the towers, when it floods into gullies or spreads across the plain, you feel its huge hands, its tremendous breast. A body that darkens with the night and knows all the fears of children, the worst sounds, the quickest path to panic.

'The solano's here.'

The ears of wheat and the olives are trembling, the nests of birds and the white lilies, men and their flocks. It comes with the feast days of St. John and Our Lady of Mount Carmel, and the Assumption of the Virgin in August. And it never brings bread, never wine, never oil. But how many of these little flowers and these trees owe their abundance to this wind? With the solano you speak only of its bad side, the side which flattens the wheat and shrivels the olives.

LA RISA DE DOLORES

Dolores habla y se ríe, come y se ríe, calla y se ríe. Le sale la risa como a una granada abierta en sazón: todo es sazón en Dolores.
—Dolores, ¿cuándo vas a dejar de reír?
Dolores farfulla algo riéndose, riéndose con los ojos, con los carrillos, con el pelo, con los brazos, riéndosele el cuerpo, farfulla algo que traducido:
—Yo no sé cuando voy a dejar de reírme.
Se ríen sus dieciocho años por todas partes, cuando está en la aceituna tirada en los suelos (con el frío que hace en la aceituna, cómo se le ponen a una las manos), cuando friega, cuando lava, cuando canta, cuando sale con el novio, le sale el chorro, la granada de su risa, le estalla abriendo a la alegría de su dentadura, chorreando en el aire el surtidor fresco de su risa.
—Yo qué sé cuando voy a dejar de reírme.

THE LAUGHTER OF DOLORES

Dolores talks and she laughs, she eats and she laughs, she's quiet and she laughs. Her laughter breaks out like a ripe open pomegranate. Everything is ripeness with Dolores.

'Dolores, when are you going to stop laughing?'

Dolores mutters something laughing, laughing with her eyes, with her cheeks, with her hair, with her arms, laughing with her body, muttering something which could be translated:

'I don't know when I will stop laughing!'

Her eighteen years are laughing everywhere; when she is collecting the olives strewn on the ground (despite the coldness of the olives when you put your hands among them), when she's scrubbing, when she's doing the washing, when she's singing, when she goes out with her boyfriend, it comes like a torrent, the explosion of her laughter, bursting from her joyous mouth, the fresh fountain of her laughter pouring into the air.

'How do I know when I will stop laughing…'

HOMBRES DEL CAMPO

Hombres del campo, hechos al polvo y a la pena, con la copla sin alegría, pardos, contra el suelo, surco va, surco viene, ya al arado, ya a la hoz o al azadón uncidos a la tierra, nobles hombres del campo, en el olvido y en la desesperanza.

Se vive como se puede, malamente; se mantiene malamente la esperanza, nadie sabe de qué.

Os sospecháis siempre cerca de la tierra, apenas os saca de ella una hora en qué el mundo se dora, el aire se hace ingrávido, la noche alegre y amáis. Luego os ata la carga del amor, se os arruga la cara, se os hace pesado el andar, duras las manos, torcida la sonrisa. No hay nada que esperar.

Al frío seguirá el calor, al relente de la noche la chicharrera del mediodía.

Y en vuestros pueblos, sobre un costerón tapiado de blanco, el lugar seguro y pobre donde la tierra que os persigue, os hará suyos para siempre.

MEN OF THE FIELDS

Men of the fields, formed by dust and sorrow, with no joy in your song; earth-coloured, earth-bound, one furrow after another, now the plough, now the sickle or the hoe, harnessed to the land, noble men of the fields, in oblivion and despair.

You live as you can, poorly, you keep hope alive, poorly; no one knows better.

Resigned to be always close to the earth, rarely stealing from it an hour in which the world becomes golden, the air lighter, the night happy, and you in love. Afterwards you are left with the burden of love, it lines your face, it makes your step heavier, your hands hard, your smile twisted. There is nothing to hope for.

Cold will follow heat, the dampness of night the chatter of cicadas at midday.

And in your villages, on a hillside walled in white, the poor sheltered place where the earth which pursues you will make you its own, forever.

III

III

LA MATALAHÚGA

La matalahúga la siembra la luna. Por marzo, cuando hace todavía frío y nadie la ve, la luna se aprovecha y la siembra. Si no, ¿de dónde la plata que es pura plata lunar de la flor, por junio? Entre el verde metálico de los maizales, entre el azulenco de los garbanzos, entre el amarillo de los nerdos, el finísimo blanco de la matalahúga. Crece la planta algo más del palmo, se corona de ramilletes redondos, comienza a cuajar el granillo, y deja por el campo un olor que se queda vagando, que viene, de pronto, a refrescar la calina. Tan delicado como el plata del color, como la hoja, como la cañilla. La matalahúga convierte las hazas en jardines, torna vergel el seco terrón veraniego, refresca tanto rastrojo, alivia de tanto amarillo en las rastrojeras. Yo la voy viendo y a mi lado oigo:

—¡Y que no valdrá poco un campo como éste!

Me quedo pensando que plata por plata, no habrá plata en el mundo que pague la que este campo representa. La matalahúga sigue inocente, finísima, desprendiendo su olor, moviéndose levemente a un dichoso vientecillo.

ANISE

The anise is sown by the moon. In March when it is still cold and no one sees her, the moon takes advantage and sows the anise. Otherwise, where does the silver of its June flowers, the pure silver of the moon, come from? Among the metallic greens of maize, the dark blues of chickpeas and the yellows of corn parsley, the delicate white of the anise. The plant grows little more than a foot high, with a crown of close-set stems, seeds begin to form, and it leaves an aroma floating in the fields that instantly refreshes the summer haze. So delicate, like the silver of its colour, like the stem and the leaf. The anise plant turns fields into gardens, makes an oasis of the dry earth of summer, refreshes so much stubble, alleviates so much yellow in the cropped fields. I am looking at it and at my side I hear:

'A field like this should really be worth something!'

It leaves me thinking, silver for silver, there is no coin in the world that could pay for what this field represents. Innocently, with great delicacy, the anise continues spreading its aroma, swaying slightly in a little current of blissful wind.

LOS VERDES

Cada verde tiene su punto. Dura poco y necesita su luz y aire propios. Estos trigos y habares, estos garbanzales: más apretado en unos, más gris, más azulenco en otros. Hay una ascensión en intensidad de color y altura de los pegujales, en esas hojas anchas, venosas, lujuriosas de los trigos, esa diversificación luego de la espiga, esa entrega pausada, llena de hermosura a la madurez, esa preñez del grano, esa obediencia al viento, primero fresca, joven, más tarde reseca y crujiente, por fin la negrura de la raspa, el amarillo total, la gracia de la plenitud, la belleza de lo cumplido.

Pocos campos de batalla como el de los haces abatidos y pocos órdenes más terribles que el que causan las segadoras en los sembrados. ¿Y no tienen como un eco de gemido de los rastrojos cuando los pisamos, un crujido que clama por toda la gloria abatida, por los días invernales de la ilusión, por el crecimiento primaveral?

Luego vendrá el arado a imponer otro orden, el de los surcos, a purificar y penitenciar la tierra para la nueva siembra.

Se cernirá una luz suave y arrepentida y, de surco en surco, saltará el pájaro picoteando el insecto extraviado y el granillo aparecido.

GREENS

Each green has its moment, lasting a short while, needing its own light and air. These fields of wheat and beans and chickpeas: the green is denser in some, in others greyer or tinged with blue. There is a mounting intensity of colour and height; in the full, veined, voluptuous leaves of the wheat, the spreading growth of the ears, the slow coming to fruition, the full splendour of maturity; the swelling of the grain, the submission to the wind; fresh and young at first, then becoming dry and crackling. And in the end, the darkness of the beards of corn, the absolute yellow, the gift of plenitude, the beauty of things fulfilled.

Few battlefields compare with those of the fallen sheaves, few states more terrible than that wrought by the reapers in the fields. And isn't there an echo of that groaning in the stubble when we walk over it, a crackling that cries out for all that fallen glory, for the illusion of winter days, for the growth of spring?

Then the plough comes to impose another order, that of the furrows; to chastise and purify the earth for the new sowing.

A soft and regretful light lingers, a bird hops from furrow to furrow, pecking at the uncovered grain and the disturbed insect.

LA PÁJARA

Por mayo se caza la pájara. Hay que aprovechar el celo del macho, diez días escasos, recién desemparejado y en estado de merecer. Se sale al alba o al trasponer el sol, con la pájara encelada, dispuesta a cantar en el primer olivo del que se cuelgue. Apenas colgada saldrá cantando y apenas cante, le responderá lejano, sorprendido, el macho que vendrá debidamente a lo suyo, con alegre premura. En un voletón raso se plantara al pie de la jaula y la pájara lo requebrará tierna, con sed de amores largamente guardados, y él se deshará en rondas y cumplidos. La pájara hará más tierno y ledo el susurro, un piñoneo apenas audible, hasta acabar engallando al galán sobre el primer terroncillo. Barrerá éste el campo con el ala baja y en ronda, para ¡ay! perder una vida que sólo para el amor nació y que fue ofrecida en sus mismas aras. La pluma sobre el cuello lacio lucirá una gota de sangre que la tierra ávida recogerá como tributo a la fecundidad perdida.

THE HEN BIRD

May is the time for trapping partridges. It has to be when the male is in rut, scarcely ten days, recently separated from his mate and in a state of eagerness.

You set out at dawn or when the sun is just setting, with the female in heat, ready to sing from the first olive tree you hang her on. She has hardly been placed there when she begins to sing and almost immediately, far off, she will be answered by the surprised male, who will come quickly, with happy urgency. Swooping low he settles down by the cage, and the female receives him with tender flattery and a thirst for love long withheld, while he circles round her proudly. Her whisperings become ever more contented and affectionate. A scarcely audible click, and the suitor is trapped on a little patch of ground. He sweeps the earth, his wings low and cramped, ending, alas, a life born solely for love, and offered up on love's altar. A drop of blood gleams on the feathers of his limp neck which the thirsty earth will receive as a tribute to lost fecundity.

LOS OLIVOS

La tierra los da sin sentirlos y ellos nunca la han traicionado, han puesto sus nervios y su dureza a su servicio. Los alberos ven olivos fruteros, siempre frescos y enramados, los cudriales los desmedran, los polvillares los asolan, pero ya puede el sol apretar, ya puede el hacha ensañarse, serles infiel la reja labradora, tardía la lluvia, duro el viento, recio el sol, agudo el frío y larga la escarcha, que puntualmente vendrán con su aceituna el año que les toque y generosamente correrá el aceite por cauchines en los molinos y blandamente se derramará en dornillos y rebanadas.

Todavía en medio de los ordenados olivares de hoy, sobresalen a veces restos de olivos viejos de casta distinta, lechines, manzanillos, injertos algunos en acebuches por las cercanías de montes y cañadas, rebajados otros, hijos de mala madre, sin orden en su conjunto, tan libres, altivos y desgreñados, tan pródigos y llenos de poesía, bailadores eternos en el campo, de un verde jugoso, con cuerpo y sombra de árboles, con acogimiento a su pie para caminantes, con menos aceituna y más leyenda que estas diligentes filas de ojiblancos que no se acaban y a quienes no detienen más que las peñas en la herrizas y los limos de los ríos donde llegan a correr. Eran aquellos olivos de molino de viga, con largos husillos de ciprés o nogal, manejados por poco más que maestro y cagarrache que duraban lo que Dios quería, porque no eran tiempos de prisa, como acomoda a los olivos que maldito el caso que hacen del tiempo.

THE OLIVE TREES

The earth brings them forth effortlessly, and they have never let her down, they have placed their nerves and their resilience at her service. Dark red soil yields fruitful trees, always fresh and thickly branched; copper-rich earth can hold them back, dry earth can blight them, but even if the sun beats down on them, if the axe treats them brutally, the blade of the plough harms them – even if the rains are late and the winds strong, the heat overwhelming, the cold severe and the frost prolonged – still, they will bring forth their olives punctually in the year of their harvesting and their oil will flow generously into the channels of the mills and pour smoothly into bowls and over cut bread.

Even among the ordered rows of today's olive trees, there are a few distinctive older olives of a different caste – *manzanilla* and *lechin* – some grafted onto wild olives close to hills and gullies; others stunted, the children of bad mothers, with nothing right in their form, so free, so dishevelled, so proud, so prodigious and so full of poetry – eternal dancers of the sierra – of a lush green, with the mass and shade of trees and a place of welcome at their feet for travellers; with fewer olives but more history than those diligent lines of pale-leafed trees that never end and are detained only by rocky ridges or the mud of riverbanks which they reach at a run. Those were the trees used for beams in the mills, with long spindles of cypress or walnut, operated only by the master miller and his assistant, which would last as long as God wished because these were not times for haste, but to allow for olive trees which don't give a curse for time.

LA FLAUTA

¿Quién le puso el nombre? La Flauta. Es igual que la tierra. Parece salida de ella. El color el mismo. Hay que cambiar surco por arruga. Y la fecundidad pareja. Todos los años su cosecha. Algo más mermada algunos, algo más opulenta otros. Todo depende, como dicen aquí, del tempero. Unas veces salen machos y otras hembras, que por variar es hermoso el mundo.

Vive en una cueva. Su marido no tiene oficio. Sale con ella, a lo que hay, que no es regular ni mucho. Vive en los campos, anda seguida de sus hijos, conoce los senderos, come cuando hay de qué, que no es siempre, en sus bordes. Bebe cuando corren, que tampoco es siempre, de los arroyos. No trabaja. ¿Para qué? Dice que no nació para trabajar, que no lo entiende, que nunca supo la relación del trabajo con la alegría o el comer. Va ligera de ropa. El oficio de andadora en campos no da para más.

Al atardecer, seguida de los suyos, tierra contra tierra, polvo y miseria, van cantando. La cueva donde viven les sirve de poco, sólo para recogerse los inviernos, cuando las noches son largas y el tiempo duro. Y eso poco se lo quitó el temporal último y ahora están a merced de los umbrales cuando llueve, del frío de las estrellas en las noches al raso.

FLAUTA *

Who named her? Flauta. She is like the earth. She seems to have sprung from it. The same colour. Only with wrinkles instead of furrows. And the same fecundity. Every year her harvest. Some more frail, some more robust. Everything depends, as they say here, on the season. Sometimes boys, sometimes girls; variety makes the world attractive.

She lives in a cave. Her husband has no job. He goes with her for whatever there is to do, which is not regular and not much. She lives in the fields, her children following, she knows the paths, she eats when there's something to eat on the verges, which is not always. She drinks when there is water in the streams, which also is not always. She doesn't work. What for? She says that she was not born to work, that she doesn't understand it, that she could never see the connection between work and happiness or eating. She wears few clothes. The office of wanderer of the fields doesn't provide for more.

When night falls, followed by her own, earth against earth, dust and misery, they go about singing. The cave where they live isn't of much use, only to huddle together in the winters when the nights are long and the weather severe. And this little was taken away by the last storm and now they are at the mercy of doorways when it rains, of the cold stars during nights in the open.

**Flauta = Flute, not translated here*

LOS TRIGOS

Eran por diciembre un leve vello de la tierra, unas briznillas que tapaban los terrones. Parecía imposible que la punta del tallo, el dedo delicado, pudiera romper la costra de la tierra endurecida con los hielos y la sequía. Y sin embargo, iba asomando como un bozo insistente, más erguido los días templados, más caído los fríos, dejando calvas donde el escardillo arañó la hoja y vino luego la helada a secarla, donde al sembrador se le fue la brazada, o el puño agarró menos grano, o donde vinieron los gorriones y los palomos que espiaban desde el tejado la ausencia del sembrador para caer sobre el campo. Luego, a las calvas las va igualando la frondosidad circundante, y aquí y allá, la tierra más generosa, el casual abono, yerguen y ennegrecen algunas matas ennoblecidas. El color de un verde tierno se va acendrando, la hoja se hace más ancha, empieza a doblarse con más gravedad a medida que las cañas engruesan. Son los primeros repasos del viento, los primeros remedos de las olas, el primer rumorcillo marinero. Ahora, con las lluvias, crece todos los días, se enmarece todos los días. Y donde la lluvia cayo con más fuerza, comienza a revolcarse. La caña aspira a espiga y las más fuertes comienzan a hacerse ásperas. Dentro de poco, aquel bozo de la tierra lamerá los ijares del caballo y cuando llegue la hora de la hoz, acariciará el hombro del segador. Pero entonces, esta lozanía sin freno, estos verdes hondos, serán sucedidos por un amarillear de dorada decadencia. Las tardes serán largas y el hombre buscará la sombra y el agua.

WHEAT

In December, it was a light down on the earth, little shoots springing up from the dry soil. It did not seem possible that the tip of the shoot, the delicate finger, could break through the surface of earth hardened by cold and by drought. Nevertheless, they kept growing like insistent bristles, stiffer on days of temperate weather, wilting a little in the cold, leaving bald patches where the hoe had taken off the leaf and the frost came and dried the ground; where the sower threw out his arm or his hand held less seed, or where the sparrows and the doves, watching from the roofs, took advantage of his absence to swoop down upon the fields. Later these bald patches will catch up with the surrounding growth, and here and there, on more fertile land, land enriched with animal excrement, they will darken and form some rich swathes. The soft green colour will heighten; the leaf become broader, begin to double over with more gravity as the stalks thicken. These are the first eddies of wind, the first suggestion of waves, the first sea-like whisperings. Now, with the rains, the wheat grows every day, becomes every day more like the sea. And where the rain falls most heavily, it starts to bend over. The stalks want to be spears of wheat, and the strongest are becoming brittle. Soon this growth rising from the earth will caress the flanks of the horses and when the time comes for the scythe it will rub the shoulders of the reapers. But by then this unrestrained vigour, these deep greens, will be followed by a yellowing of golden decadence. The afternoons will be long, and men will seek shade and water.

NICOLÁS EL HISTORIADOR

Estos caminos lo conocían bien y lo echan de menos. Como que por él sabía su propia historia. Lo mismo que la casa y los olivos: sabia el cuento de todo este contorno y no se le caía de los labios. Venía, viejo como ya estaba, con el bastoncillo y el pasito entrecortado, casi todos los días y comenzaba:
—Cuando se hizo este cortijo...
Y seguía:
—Cuando corrió este agua por primera vez...
Y la palabra morosa traía días y figuras.
—Aquí había un cortijo viejo y un día llegaron los amos y el maestro Esperavanes y dijo el amo: Yo haría un cortijo así y así. Y lo pintó con el bastón en el suelo. El maestro Esperavanes lo copió en un papel y al día siguiente comenzaron a derribar el cortijo viejo y a levantar el nuevo.
El pobre Nicolás se murió este invierno. Se lo llevó una madrugada de febrero, cruda e inmóvil. Tenía prisa. La prisa de los viejos. Fue mucha gente al entierro. Estas cosas perdieron su cuento y su cantor... Y yo echo de menos el paso leve de mi madre joven y de nosotros niños en su relato.

NICOLÁS THE HISTORIAN

These paths knew him well and will miss him. It was through him they knew their own history. The same with the house and the olive fields: he knew the whole story of this place and he would never stop telling it. He came almost every day, old man that he was then, with his stick and his short step, and began:

'When they built this farmhouse…'

And he went on:

'When the water flowed for the first time…'

And these slow words brought back people and past days.

'There was an old farmhouse here and one day the owner came with the head builder Esperavanes, and the owner said: I would make a farmhouse like this and this. And he drew it with his stick in the earth. The head builder, Esperavanes, copied it onto a piece of paper and the next day they began to pull down the old farmhouse and build the new.'

Poor Nicolás died this winter. He was taken away early one morning in February, raw and still. He was in a hurry, the haste of the old. There were many people at his burial. These things will lose their stories and their storyteller… And I miss the light step of my young mother and of us, as children, in his telling.

EL PRIMER SOPLO
DEL OTOÑO

Todavía en agosto, a pesar de la chicharra y de que apenas hay algún braván en los rastrojos, de que siguen las tórtolas y de que aún no han comenzado a acordonarse las golondrinas en los alambres. A pesar de todo, algo indefinible en el tacto del aire, algo en su olor, como un primer soplo del otoño.

Se abren las granadas, y en la frondosidad de los melonares, entre el fruto monstruoso, alguna tardía flor amarilla y diminuta. La mazorca grana, la aceituna engorda. La gente del campo no teme más que al solano. En cuanto la sierra cubre su cresta con un filillo algodonoso, tiemblan. Porque al doblar el día, todo manazas y calentones, hurtando donde puede, el solano de agosto.

A los días se les nota el cansancio. En las últimas eras hay que dormir arropados, porque las noches, al alargarse, se enfrían. Va siendo la hora del braván, de que los membrillos colmen el aire con su aroma y de que caiga el primer fruto de los nogales.

Pronto —el corazón lo anticipa todo— el otoño irá sacando sus tintas suaves y volverá a ser grato pasear por los senderos, entre tierras olientes a recién abiertas y mojadas.

THE FIRST BREATH OF AUTUMN

Before the end of August, despite the cicadas and hardly a plough in fields of stubble, and the turtle doves still here, and the swallows not yet lined up on the wires; in spite of all this, there is something indefinable in the touch of the air, something in its aroma, like a first breath of autumn.

The pomegranates are opening and in the tangled vegetation of the melon beds, amongst the monstrous fruit, there are a few tiny and late yellow flowers. Corncobs are ripening, the olives are swelling, and country people fear only the solano. When the crest of the sierra is covered by a thin cottony thread, they tremble. Because before the day has turned, stealing into every corner, stifling and bothersome, the solano of August.

You notice the fatigue of these days. For the last of the threshing, you have to sleep wrapped up because the nights are lengthening and getting colder. The time for the plough is coming when the fragrance of quinces fills the air and the first fruit falls from the walnut trees.

Soon – the heart anticipates everything – autumn will bring out its soft tints and once again it will be pleasant to walk along paths beside earth recently opened and moist and odorous.

MIGUELILLO SE VA

Miguelillo se ha ido. Se lo han llevado de porquero, lejos. Dicen que lloraba porque no quería y no lo dejaron despedirse. Lo echamos mucho de menos, en su humildad, en su silencio, en su servicio. Miguelillo estaba con los pavos, olivares arriba, olivares abajo. Dormía hecho un ovillo. Tenía los ojos alegres y siempre estaba contento. Se lo han llevado a un campo de jarales y adelfas, retamas y un río. Los pavos que lo conocían y aguardaban que pasara la siesta para su merodeo diario, lo echaban de menos. Se apelotonan junto a la puerta, esperándolo. Y Miguelillo andará lejos, entre sus jaras y sus adelfas.

MIGUELILLO IS GOING AWAY

Miguelillo has gone. They've taken him off to be a swineherd, far away. They say he cried because he didn't want to go and they wouldn't let him say his goodbyes. We miss him a lot, for his humility, his quietness, his sense of duty. Miguelillo minded the turkeys, up and down the olive fields. He slept curled up in a ball. He had happy eyes and was always contented. They have taken him to a place of rockroses and oleander, of gorse and a river. The turkeys that knew him and used to wait until after his siesta for their daily outing miss him most. They are lining up beside the door, waiting for him. And little Miguel will be far away, amongst his rockroses and his oleander.

LOS RASTROJOS ARDEN

Estas hogueras de los rastrojos, se me antojan el sacrificio final al terrible dios del verano. Se alargan los festones de llamas por el atardecer, acendrándose en la oscuridad, estallando donde el forraje tuvo más cuerpo, atenuándose donde la mies anduvo mermada. Se llena el aire de un olor que compendia todos los del verano. La última espiral de humo viene a confundirse con la primera nubecilla otoñal. Al entrar en el patio, ya atardecido, los dompedros abren su olor más concentrado que nunca, fresco y natural. Con la cercanía del otoño huelen siempre más tiernamente los dompedros. La sequía lo va agostando todo. Apenas cae un hilillo de agua en la alberca. El campo comienza a recogerse. Los tordos vienen a los higos tardíos y a las uvas primeras. Los vencejos hacen su ronda de despedida y se presienten los primeros zorzales. Las tórtolas escasean y se levantan claras las bandadas de palomos. Han vuelto los abejarucos y han caído sobre el colmenar, afligido con la castra reciente.

Ya cabe sentarse sin sombra y acechar en la tarde la salida de la luna por un cielo ceniciento, y sobre un campo que sólo espera las primeras lluvias para volver a la dulzura. Pronto habrá que arroparse y sentir la delicia del frío fuera, del dulce calor dentro.

THE STUBBLE IS BURNING

These bonfires of stubble seem to me the last sacrifice to the terrible god of summer. The ribbons of fire spread at dusk, distinct in the darkness, flaring up where the wheat was dense and dying down where the growth was less. The air is filled with all the aromas of summer. The last wisps of smoke mingle with the first little clouds of autumn. Coming into the patio at a late hour, the 'four o'clock' flowers are opening, their scent, fresh and natural, more pungent than ever. With the coming of autumn, the scent of 'four o'clocks' is always sweeter. Drought affects everything. There is scarcely a trickle of water in the cistern. The earth is gathering itself. The blackbirds are at the late figs and the first grapes. The swifts are making their rounds of goodbyes and we are expecting the first thrushes. There are fewer turtle doves and flocks of pigeons are rising clear in the air. The bee-eaters have returned and swooped on hives already suffering after the recent pruning.

Now you can sit in the evening without needing shade and wait for the moon to appear in an ashen sky above land that only awaits the first rains to become mellow once again. Soon it will be necessary to wrap up and enjoy the delights of the cold outside, the sweet warmth within.

SE CAE LA ACEITUNA

Siempre, por este mes, al solano último de agosto, a la lluvia temprana, al calor postrero y apretado, comienza a caerse la aceituna. De buenas a primeras, una mañana, aparecen inexplicablemente los primeros puntillos verdes sobre el suelo del olivo, tersos al principio, encogiéndose rápidamente, hasta quedar en hueso mondo y lirondo.

La caída de la aceituna siempre llega por los mismos días, repicando a otoño, entreabriendo molinos, empujando a los calores finales, a las tórtolas y golondrinas atrasadas, dejando el aire vacante para tordos y estorninos, avisando con el cobre primero a las hojas, para la partida. Sabe a lluvia que no va a tardar, a neblina primera, a sol pálido. Las últimas moras están a punto. El vallado las ofrece a cientos. Ya no queda un maizal en pie, y el viento barre los últimos melonares.

Surco a surco, el braván va borrando el amarillo del campo, vistiéndolo de colores severos, blanquecino en los alberos, rojizo en los polvillares, grisáceo en los riquísimos bujeos. Ya nadie duerme al raso y los primeros escalofríos comienzan a pedir las primeras candelas.

THE OLIVES ARE FALLING

Always in this month, with the last winds of August, and early rain, in the final suffocating heat, the olives begin to fall. One morning, with no warning and for no reason, the first tiny green dots appear on the earth below the trees, smooth-skinned at first, then rapidly shrivelling until there is nothing left but the stone, bald and bare.

The olives always fall on the same days, announcing autumn, half-opening the olive mills; chasing away the last waves of heat, the turtle doves and late swallows, leaving the sky for starlings and thrushes, the first copper-coloured leaves suggesting it is time to depart. You know it won't be long before rain comes, the first mists, a pale sun. The last berries are ready for picking. The hedgerows offer them in hundreds. There are no longer any cornstalks upright in the fields and the wind is raking the last beds of melons.

Furrow by furrow, the plough is erasing the yellow of the fields, dressing them in austere colours, pale white on ochre fields, dusty reds on more sandy ground, closer to grey on darker, richer soil. No one sleeps outside now, and the first chills begin to suggest the first fires.

EL PENSADOR

El Pensador se ha muerto.

Dicen que se sintió malillo de pronto y como creía que era nada se fue sin despedirse. Luego no tuvo tiempo. Le vino tan corto que a poco de llegar a su casa se encontró con la muerte que parecía haberlo citado allí.

Esta noche en la cuadra se notaba su ausencia. Los mulos que lo conocían bien, hallaban no sé que extraño en la nueva y no acostumbrada mano que les servía el pienso. Había más impaciencia en el relincho que corría por los pesebres, un natural presentimiento de que algo le faltaba al día para acabar como todos.

Yo bajaba muchas noches a echar un párrafo con él, acompasado por el roer de los mulos.

—Cada uno tiene lo que tiene, solía decir. Ya ve usted, las mujeres no se hacen a gusto. Unas entienden y otras no. Unas entienden con palabras, otras con palos. Algunas ni con lo uno ni con lo otro. ¿Y qué hace usted? ¡Si siquiera pudiera uno dejarlas! Pero ?quién las deja? Y menos un pobre.

Y luego añadía como si se tratara de lo mismo:

—¡Qué buenos se están poniendo los mulos!

THE STABLE BOY

Our stable boy has died.

They say he felt a little ill all of a sudden, and because he thought it was nothing, he left us without saying goodbye. Afterwards he had no time. Death came to him so quickly, just after he had got home, as if it had an appointment with him there.

You could sense his absence in the stables that night. The mules which had known him well found something strange in the new and unaccustomed hand which gave them their feed. There was more restiveness about the braying of the animals in their stalls, a natural presentiment that on this day something was missing to make it end like other days.

There were many nights when I would go down to chat with him, to the accompaniment of the champing of the mules.

'Each one has its own way', he used to say, 'you know, women aren't made as we would like. Some of them understand but others don't. Some get it with words, others need the stick. Some will never understand either way. But what can you do? If you could just leave them. But who would leave them? Certainly not a poor man like me.'

And afterwards he added, as if continuing in the same vein:

'How well the mules are doing'.

IV

IV

EL CORAZÓN Y
EL CAMPO

EL corazón discurre sobre estos campos. Lo llevan los ojos, los oídos, el olfato. Se hace sentido. Lo sabe, lo acecha todo, lo espera todo, se tiende sobre la tierra, se abriga entre dos surcos, pasa entre los olivos. La belleza es un vuelo. ¿Quién lo dijo? No se está quieta en las cosas y no se mueve de ellas. Dentro y fuera. ¿Cómo decirlo? Parece que somos pozos oscuros, hondos, donde nada llega. Y asomándonos, está todo. La loma, el peñascal, la vera de la zanja, la desazón, la felicidad acechadora, la alegría que apunta, la sombra cernida. ¡Ay corazón, lento y oscuro!

Enero es bellísimo. Va abriendo día a día, surco a surco, secretos al campo. El campo es una inmensa caja de secretos. Hay que saber verlos. Espiarlos hasta que nos los entregue. Así, yendo de pronto, el simple color de una piedra junto a la que pasamos mil veces sin repararla, la forma de un árbol, la luz de un camino.

Todo va quedando. Lo mismo que la hoja caduca sobre el sembrado añadirá lozanía al tallo, lustre a la hoja, cargazón a la espiga. El sol de esta tarde está creando dentro y fuera, en alma y tierra, calor, sin que nunca acabe enteramente de morir. ¿Qué muere? Todo esto sigue. Y el sonar del campo, del río, entre estas riberas de cielo hermosísimas, deja un largo eco, una llamada eterna a la belleza.

THE HEART AND THE COUNTRY

The heart hastens over these fields, carried by the eyes, the ears, the sense of smell. It gives meaning. It knows, watching everything, awaiting everything, stretching out over the land, sheltering between two furrows, passing amongst the olive trees. Beauty is flight. Who said that? It doesn't come to rest in things, and it doesn't move from them. Inside and outside. How can one describe it? It seems as if we are deep dark wells, where nothing reaches. And yet all things are looking over us. The low ridges, the rocky crags, the banks of watercourses, anxiety, happiness lying in wait, joy breaking forth, shadows encroaching. Oh heart, dark and slow!

January is so beautiful. Day by day, furrow by furrow, it is opening the secrets of the fields. The land is an immense box of secrets. You have to know how to see them. To wait and watch until they reveal themselves. Thus, being aware, suddenly, of the pure colour of a stone we go by a thousand times without noticing, the shape of a tree, the light of a path.

Everything remains, just as the leaf fallen on the field after sowing nourishes the stalks, adds lustre to the leaves and body to the ears of wheat. The late afternoon sun is creating warmth, within and without, in the soul and on the land, without ever quite dying down. What dies? All this continues. And the sound of the fields, of the river, between these banks of ravishing sky, leaves a long echo, a never-ending call to beauty.

LOS ACEITUNEROS

Desde lejos son unos humos lentos sobre los olivares. Acercándose, un rumor disperso. Voces, alguna copla, el ruido de un banco que se cierra, el manoteo rápido sobre las hojas, el aleteo del aventador, la caída continua y mullida de la aceituna, como una cascada negra, en los sacos. Pocas veces hará la tierra más suyos a los hombres que en las aceitunerías. Aceituna arrugada, verde, vinosa, al igual que los rostros, que las ropas, que las manos enterronadas. Salen de mañana arrecidos, se reparten por el olivar, atacan a los árboles, recogen ávidamente el fruto, izan las canastas sobre las testas. Van las aceituneras pardas, sucias, apenas los ojos brillantes entre los pañuelos, apenas salvándose la gracia de una forma bajo los pantalones. Los olivos se les entregan y revierten las ramas despojadas a la altivez de antes, a esperar la nueva flor que el aire les tiene guardada. Y los aceituneros siguen camada adelante, a lo suyo, oscuros, torpes, implacables. Aquí lo humano no guarda par con lo sereno del día, con la paz, con la limpieza del aire. Todo se vuelve afán, prisa, que nada quede. El rumor pasa y tras él quedan enhiestos los ramones, quieto el aire. Y la madre grita:

—Y que el niño no se vaya a quedar atrás.

Y el niño viene bamboleándose, aburridillo, sin comprender muy bien todo aquello, agradecido al solecito de enero, después del frío inexplicable de la noche antes.

THE OLIVE PICKERS

From a distance they seem wreaths of smoke moving slowly over the olive fields. Nearer, scattered sounds. Voices, a snatch of song, a workbench being folded, the rapid shaking of leaves, the beating with winnowing forks, the continuous muffled fall, the dark cascade of olives into sacks. Seldom does the land so merge with its workers as at the time of olive-picking. The olives, green, wrinkled, vinous, like the faces, the clothes, the earthy hands. They set off in the morning stiff with cold, spread out in the olive field, attack the trees and energetically collect the fruit, hoisting the baskets onto their heads. The women are dark-coloured and dirty, their shining eyes scarcely showing amongst their rags, the grace of their bodies scarcely apparent in their trousers. The trees surrender their olives and the shorn branches spring up again, to await the new flower the air has been saving for them. And the olive pickers move onwards together, in their own way, dark, awkward, unstoppable. Here the activity of man is out of step with the quiet of the day, with the peacefulness, with the purity of the air. Everything is strained, done quickly, so that nothing is left. The clamour passes, leaving branches upright again, the air undisturbed. And the mother shouts:

'Don't let the child fall behind.'

And the child comes running erratically, a bit bored, not understanding much of all that, enjoying the little sun of January after the unaccountable cold of the night before.

LABRANZA

Por este tiempo pisándoles los talones a los aceituneros, yuntas y taladores. Después de las lluvias de invierno, las tierras no demasiado pegadizas suelen estar buenas y no enlutan la reja que entra bien y con fruto. Así, el primer brotar de la yerba que es el más temible, se corta al romper y hay mucho adelantado. Ya se adivinan jaramagos, lenguazas, las yerbas todas de nombres ignorados. Los taladores van haciendo lo suyo. Los olivos, tras de dar fruto y leña, aparecen más jóvenes y ascéticos, más en brazos del cielo y de la tierra. Se cruzan los barbechos y se preparan para las siembras de primavera. Aquí nunca se empieza ni acaba. El campo es el cuento de nunca acabar.

WORKING THE LAND

At this time, treading on the heels of the olive pickers, come teams for ploughing and pruning. After the winter rains, earth which is not too muddy is ready, it doesn't bury the plough which digs in well with good results. So, the first growth of weeds, which is the most feared, is cut as it breaks through and much time is gained. Now you start to see charlock and spurge, all the grasses with names we don't know. The tree pruners set to work. The olives, after giving fruit and firewood, seem younger, more ascetic, more in the embrace of earth and sky. Fallow fields are exchanged and prepared for the spring sowing. Here nothing begins or ends. The land is the story that never ends.

EL OJIBLANCAR

¡Oh viejo olivar! Cinco fanegas de tierra mal contadas, unos rimeros de olivos viejos, y ¡cuanta belleza! Poca aceituna y alguna leña. Los troncos negruzcos, agrietados, retorcidos, enjutísimos, nadie sabe cómo sostienen los ramones tiernos, la hoja brillante, la flor en abril, la aceituna en agosto. Hijos del resol, sujetos a toda helada, maltratados de años y hachas, añadiendo todavía hermosura al paisaje.

Dicen las gentes:

—Poco le queda ya al Ojiblancar, si se quiere que la leña valga algo.

O:

—¡Lastima de tierra!

O:

—¡Con lo que valen ahora las leñas!

Y ellos, duros, sin oír las voces, siguen enviando por la vena viva, entre la leña muerta, un hilo de savia que mantiene el verde saludable. Parecen dolor cuajado. Las tórtolas los aman, y en cuanto llega la primavera, la flor los torna jóvenes. Ya nadie se acuerda de quien puso el Ojiblancar, ni de qué manos abrieron sus hoyos, ni cuáles talaron sus primeros ramones. Sólo este poco de belleza queda de cuanto trajinaron en la tierra.

Y, sin embargo, el talador ha medido los olivos con sus ojillos grises, se ha echado el hacha al hombro, los ha vuelto a medir, y se ha ido murmurando que allí no tiene nada que hacer.

THE OLD OLIVE GROVE

Oh, the old olive grove! A clump of old trees, an acre more or less of land, and so much beauty! Few olives and little wood. The trunks blackened, split, twisted, dried up; no one knows how they can support the tender branches, the flashing leaves, the blossom in April and the olives in August. Children of the burning sun, exposed to every frost, mistreated by the axe and the years, yet still bringing beauty to the landscape.

Country people say:

'Little remains now in the old olive grove, though perhaps the wood has some value'.

Or,

'A disgrace to the land!'

Or,

'With what wood is worth nowadays!'

But they're tough, they don't listen, they continue sending a trickle of sap through a vein still living in the dead wood, which keeps the green in health. They seem the essence of pain. The turtle doves love them, and as soon as spring arrives, the blossom turns them young again. Now no one remembers who planted the old grove, whose hands opened up the earth, or pruned the first branches. Only this little beauty remains from so much activity on the land.

Yet, nevertheless, the pruner has taken the measure of these olive trees with his narrow grey eyes, and shouldered his axe, and examined them again, and gone off murmuring there is nothing to be done here.

EL TALADOR

¡Cómo están los ramones! ¡Un tallo así llevan! Y el hombre corta el brazo desde el codo y señala. El hombre que no trata más que a los olivos y que es ya casi un olivo. Cuando los va talando les habla, les explica por qué hay que cortar esta rama, por qué hay que remeter aquélla, por qué hay que perdonar esa otra. Brazos, piel, ojos, son de olivo: color de olivo los ojillos.

—La gente me engañara. Lo que tiene, los olivos no me engañan. Ya verá el año que viene.

Va entre ellos como entre familia. Les cuenta lo que le pasa, la hija que se le va a casar, la mujer que con nada tiene bastante, el nietecillo que esta ya echando los dientes, lo que le falta para comprar la casa.

Lleva encasquetado el sombrero, trata al hacha como a una hija más. La trama se va esponjando, está poniendo a punto de temblor el olivar.

—¡Qué tiernos están! Dentro de nada como la nieve. Como los olivos, un olivo más, hablándoles, acariciándoles, alma de olivo, en paciencia, en generosidad, en humildad, el talador en su reino.

THE PRUNER
OF THE OLIVE TREES

'How are these branches? They should be this high!'

And the man crooks his arm at the elbow to demonstrate. The man who works only with the olives and has almost become an olive tree himself. When he is pruning, he talks to them, explaining why this branch has to be cut, why this one needs to be done again, why this one is to be spared. Arms, skin, eyes like the olive tree; the pupils of his eyes the colour of the olives.

'People will let me down, but not the olive trees. You'll see in the coming year.'

He goes amongst them as if amongst family. He tells them what is happening to him, the daughter who is about to get married, the wife who never has enough, the little grandchild who is already teething, what he still needs to buy the house.

He wears his hat pulled down low, holds his axe like another child. The flowers are opening, the olive field is on the point of trembling.

'How tender they are, in no time they will be like snow.'

One more tree amongst the others, talking to them, stroking them; soul of the olive tree, in patience, generosity, humility; the olive pruner in his kingdom.

LAS HELADAS

Siempre, en estos meses, se vive con el temor a la helada. Es una muerte nocturna y segura que viene todos los años a hacer de las suyas. Trae poco y se lleva lo que puede, aceituna o pegujal. Hija de los cielos serenos y de las noches claras, invisible y extensa, deja su huella por los campos, blancos al amanecer, aterida la planta, encogido el fruto.

—¡Buena ha caído esta noche!

Y el resuello humea en el aire. No hay quien se asome a la puerta. Les tiembla todo el mundo.

Las manda, sin duda, el hielo durísimo de las estrellas a besar la tierra, en unas nupcias tremendas, que detienen la vida, en medio del silencio de la noche. Su cuerpo de amante inmenso y mortal, queda extendido en desolación y blancura sobre el campo.

Por las mañanas no hay quien se mueva. Se engarrotan hombres y plantas. Todo va hacia los adentros. El pegujal se encepa, busca el calorcillo interior de la tierra, echa su fuerza hacia abajo. La aceituna sin madurar se avinata y empequeñece, y la cortedad de los días no da tiempo al sol de rodear los olivos y deja en su lado norte que la helada de una noche aguarde a la de otra.

—¡La que va a caer!

Y el cielo está impasible, preparándose. Y apenas oscurecido, con las últimas luces y las primeras estrellas, invisible, sobre la tierra inerme, sobre la plantilla recién despuntada, sobre la flor que se adelantó y el caminante retrasado, sobre las aves, comenzará a caer la helada.

Mañana se hallaran dondequiera sus despojos. Y hombres y animales se anunciarán con una larga vaharada. Sobre el paisaje se cernirá un halo, un velo de niebla que hará fantásticas las perspectivas, tiernas las lejanías, íntimo el campo.

FROSTS

Always, in these months, we live with the fear of frost. It is a death, nocturnal and certain, returning every year to take its toll, bringing little but taking what it can, olives or crops. Child of calm skies and clear nights, imperceptible and extensive, leaving its imprint on the fields; white at dawn, the plants rigid, the fruit shrivelled.

'Well, it really came down last night!'

And breath becomes smoke in the air. No one wants to go to the door. The whole world is shivering.

No doubt these frosts are sent from the hardest ice of the stars to embrace the earth in a terrible union which arrests life, in the middle of the silence of the night. Its lover's body, immense and deathly, extended in desolation and whiteness on the land.

In the mornings no one moves. Men and plants are rigid. Everything turns inward. The crops become like vines, seeking the little warmth still in the earth, using their strength to push down. The olives, still immature, become desiccated and shrivel and the shortness of days allows no time for the sun to reach round the trees leaving their north-facing side frozen until the next night.

'It's really going to come down!'

And the sky remains impassive, preparing itself. And hardly has it become dark, with the last lights and the first stars, when frost will begin to fall, invisible, on the inert land, on the first growth of crops, on early flowers, on birds and late travellers.

Tomorrow will reveal its effects wherever one looks. And men and animals will declare themselves with their vaporous breath. A halo will wrap the landscape, a veil of mist will make the vistas fantastic, distances softer, the land intimate.

FINALES DE ENERO

Enero es así. Con días como esté da gloria. Está todo tan limpio, tan lavado el aire, tan recién vestidas tierras y sierras, todo estrenándose. La tierra estrenándose. No hay apenas planta de hombre, huella de animal; sólo, aquí y allá, aparece el aire turbado por la candela de algún talador o aceitunería. Ni apenas pájaros. Alguna avefría silenciosa, alguna primilla a lo suyo, dos lentos grajos. Todo se está quieto. Los caminos perdidos con las lluvias últimas y el agua derramándose sin uso y sin tasa, por zanjas y regueras, hace más solo el campo con su rumor. Bella, mineral y fría. Contra el verde tierno del vallado, contra el verde duro y eterno de los olivos, los árboles que perdieron las hojas, hacen como un humo vagoroso. Y donde hay un almendro, hay un poquito de luz que es un temblor. ¿Un temblor? ¿Una música? El aire está delicado alrededor del almendro. Dentro de unos días, cuando menos se espere, temblará. Ahora abriga la sierra unos colores increíbles, hondos, morados, verdes, un vaho de ternura que la ciñe. Ya estarán a punto los primeros lirios entre las grietas de roca con tierra mullida, los primeros narcisos silvestres con su enorme olor.

LATE JANUARY

January is like this. On these days it gives such pleasure. Everything is so fresh, the air so cleansed, the sierras and the land so recently clothed, everything dressed up. The land in its new clothes. There is hardly any trace of man or track of animals, the air only disturbed, here and there, by the fires of a woodcutter or the olive pickers. And hardly any birds. A silent lapwing, a kestrel hunting, two slow-moving rooks. Everything keeps still. The paths erased by the recent rains, the water running off uselessly, to no purpose, through ditches and channels, making the fields more solitary with its murmur. Beautiful, mineral and cold. The trees which have lost their leaves are wreathlike against the fresh green on the slopes and the hard and eternal green of the olives. And where there is an almond tree there is a little light, like a trembling. Trembling? Music? The air around the almond tree is delicate. In a few days, when least expected, it will tremble. Now the sierra is covered with astonishing colours, deep purples and greens, an aura of sweetness envelops it. The first irises are about to flower in the soft earth in cracks between rocks, and the first wild narcissi with their huge scent.

LOS ZORZALES
NO VIENEN

Este año no hay zorzales.

Miguel está desesperado. Es un labrador sin cosecha. Se pasa el día espiando el aire, por si vienen, pero el aire sigue imperturbable, bellísimo, sin asomo de pájaro. Miguel pasa y repasa sus perchas. Los zorzales son su pan del invierno. ¿En qué remoto norte se habrán quedado? ¿De quienes dependerán sus pasaportes?

Y es lo que dice Miguel:

—Para que se vea: el año pasado tan poca aceituna y tantos zorzales: doce, catorce cada día. No daban las perchas abasto. Y éste, tanta aceituna y tan pocos zorzales. Con lo gordos que se pondrían.

No hay quien lo entienda —dice Miguel y tiene razón.

Y añade:

—Son las tormentas, las tormentas.

Y se queda tan tranquilo con la explicación. Es lo que necesitaba para su tranquilidad: una explicación.

THE THRUSHES
ARE NOT COMING

This year there are no thrushes.

Miguel is desperate. He is a farm worker with no harvest. He spends the day looking into the air in case they come; but the air remains undisturbed, so beautiful, with no sign of the bird. Miguel checks his snares and checks them again. The thrushes are his winter fare. In what remote north have they been detained? Who is responsible for their passports?

And it is as Miguel says:

'It's like this. Last year, so few olives and so many thrushes, twelve, fourteen every day. There were hardly enough traps. And this year, so many olives and so few thrushes. And how well fed they could be!

'No one understands why', says Miguel, and he's right.

And he adds: 'It's the storms, the storms.'

And he's so happy with this explanation. It's what he needed for his peace of mind, an explanation.

LOS MULOS

¿Quién os ha cantado, fieles trabajadores?
Nadie ha reparado en vuestros ojos inteligentes, en vuestra paciente fortaleza, en vuestra segura seriedad.
Os conocen los olivares, duros como vosotros, constantes en el surco y la besana, sufridos al ubio, al sol y a la sed, en este perenne zurcido de la tierra que hacéis con el arado. ¡Como conocéis la voz, la ocasión del esfuerzo, el lugar del descanso, la hora del pienso!
Por la noche, me gusta bajar a la cuadra, caliente estos meses de invierno con los vahos húmedos, y pasar ante la fila de cabezas, largas las orejas, dulces los ojos maliciosos. Me gusta acariciar las testas enormes, los belfos suaves, oír el roer acompasado.
Y al llegar a un pesebre, dejar que una cabezota se me pare en el hombro, y se me quede en él, pesando como una inesperada cargazón de ternura.

THE MULES

Who has sung your praises, faithful workers?

No one has paid attention to your intelligent eyes, your patient fortitude, your reliable seriousness.

The olive fields, as tough as you, know you; always there, in field and furrow, enduring under the yoke, in sun and in thirst, in the continuous stitching of the land you make with the plough. How do you know the voice, the moment for strength, the place of rest, the hour for fodder?

At night I like to go down to the stables, warmed in these winter months with humid breaths, and pass along the line of heads, the long ears and the sweet malicious eyes. I like to stroke the huge heads, the thick, soft lips, to hear the rhythmic chomping.

And when I stop by a stall, to allow a large head to rest on my shoulder, and stay there, heavy with an unexpected burden of tenderness.

TORNAN LOS ABEJARUCOS

Han vuelto los abejarucos.

Uno, dos, un silbido, un vuelo, tornamos los ojos. ¿dónde estamos? La tarde bellísima, la novia de la tierra, o tan quieta como una monja en oración. La tarde bellísima, el calor incipiente mezclado a frescores tardíos, la sutil línea de las montañas, las maravillas del morado, del gris más encendido, más opaco, de su color; tanto árbol dispuesto a la juventud, tanta hoja a la danza, tanto pico dislocado.

Y la rueda del año serena, eterna, en su giro debido, en su momento justo, nos devuelve, velocísimo, anunciador, terror de la abejuela, el abejaruco.

Algo vuelve dentro de nosotros todas las primaveras, algo que nos rejuvenece como a estos viejos árboles, como a estos perdidos cortijos, como a esta fija y eterna esperanza.

THE BEE-EATERS ARE BACK

The bee-eaters have come back.

One, two, a call, a flight, we turn our eyes. Where are we? The loveliest evening, the bride of the earth or quiet as a nun at prayer. The loveliest evening, the rising heat mingling with late breezes, the fine line of the mountains, and the colours, the wonderful purples, the brightest and densest of greys. So many trees affecting youthfulness, so many leaves dancing, so many open beaks.

And the wheel of the year, calm, eternal, in its necessary cycle, brings back to us, at the right moment, at great speed, the harbinger, tormentor of the hive, the bee-eater.

Something comes back within us every spring, something that rejuvenates us, like those old trees, like those ruined farmhouses, like this fixed and eternal hopefulness.

LAS ABEJAS EN LOS TILOS

¡Quién fuera abeja! ¡Quién fuera abeja para no perderse una, ésta quiero, ésta no quiero, aquí me entretengo, en la otra me columpio! Sobre todo cuando los tilos florecen, meterse follaje adentro, estar en la penumbra verde clara y olvidarse.

Como si no hubiera colmenas en el mundo, sino sólo este aroma, este color, este ir muriendo en la delicia, sin notarlo, muriendo, muriendo, viendo abajo los arriates con las rosas, las amapolas, los granados en flor, la viña con los racimillos despuntando, la tapia blanca y los olivos que lo llenan todo fuera, serenos, ordenados, las tierras verdegueando con las primeras siembras primaverales, la línea de las sierras, el cielo, el cielo.

¡Quién fuera abeja estas tardes, cuando los tilos florecen y la sangre va por las venas, respondiendo al latido del aire, una con él, caliente, esperanzada, colgada sobre el tiempo, ay, sobre el tiempo, colmena que todo lo quiere para él!

THE BEES IN THE LIME TREES

Who wouldn't be a bee! Who wouldn't be a bee so as not to miss anything; I want this one, I don't want that one, here I'll stay awhile, in the other I'll swing! Above all, when the lime trees are flowering, to step inside the blossom, to be in the clear green shade and forget oneself.

As if there were no hives in the world, only this colour, this scent, this dying in delight, and not to notice it, dying, dying; seeing the verges below with roses, poppies, pomegranates in flower, the vines with clusters of grape berries, the white wall, and the olive trees spreading over everything beyond, serene, ordered; the land becoming green with the first spring sowing, the line of the mountains, the sky, the sky.

Who wouldn't be a bee on these afternoons when the lime trees are in flower and blood goes through the veins, responding to the pulsing of the air, becoming one with it, warm, full of hope, suspended over time; alas, over time, the hive that covets everything for itself!

TIERRA ETERNA

Sola y eterna, tierra de arados, de sementeras y de olivar, mil veces regada con sudores de hombres, con cuidados, con maldiciones, con desesperaciones de hombres, hermosura diaria, espejo y descanso nuestro.

Nunca cansas, siempre lista, inscrita una y otra vez por hierros y por huellas, volcada por rejas al sol y a la lluvia, a todo tempero, siempre con la dádiva conforme al trabajo, medida a nuestros huesos.

¡Ay de los que te olvidaren, de los que en su piel y en sus ojos pierdan tu recuerdo, de los que no se refresquen contigo, de los que te pierdan de alma!

ETERNAL EARTH

Eternal and unique, land of ploughs, of crops and olive fields; watered a thousand times by the sweat of men, with care, with curses, with the despair of men; splendour of each day, our mirror and our rest.

Never tired, always ready, scored again and again by tools and tracks; turned over by the plough in sun and rain, in every season, the reward always matching the effort, measure of our bones.

Woe to those who forget you, who lose your memory on their skin and in their eyes, those who fail to replenish themselves in you, those who lose you in their soul!

AUTHOR'S INTRODUCTION
to the 1976 edition published by Destino

Some rain has fallen since I wrote this book some thirty years ago now. Not always as those working the land would have wished, more and unseasonal than at times suited them. Thirty years are a gust of wind and like a gust of wind they have gone, but we would have to multiply this figure many times if we wanted to make an account of the changes that have taken place in their passing. I can see this if I look up from reading these pages to the same fields nearby, about which they were written. There have been more and greater changes than years. As with all change something has been lost and something gained, in varying proportion according to events and circumstances. Some of the 'things' in this book no longer exist. Some of the people written about here have not only passed away but their roles and their tasks are no longer known. With some of the characters I have chanced to meet during these years I have had to rub my eyes to convince myself that they were the same flesh and bones, and not just figures of my imagination.

Crazy Juanillo for example, on horseback one day in the olive fields:

'Can it be you, Juanillo?'

'Si, Señor, it is me.'

I didn't know if he came out of the fields or out of the book. The same in the way he hurried off to nothing in particular, in the gesture as he went his own way, nothing more.

'What are you doing?'

'The same as ever, looking after the olives, there is no one else to keep an eye on them.'

A little greyer and without his old cord jacket, he went off talking as loudly as ever, leaving me marvelling once again at the most delicate line that separates fiction from reality. On the other hand, Miguelillo, who used to look after the turkeys, presented himself to me as a fully grown man wearing a jacket of fine leather and in his new car.

'I bought it in Germany.'

'But Miguel…'

'I've come back to marry and as soon as I've done that I'll be off again'.

'But really, Miguel…'

'Take advantage when you can, it won't last long.'

Narciso the Singer and Flauta are both dead. The night watcher and stable boy and their jobs are no more. The mules are no longer there, the stables empty, without the sound of their chomping. Only one pair remain now, for show. The white poplars down at the river have come down as they were obstructing the water channels; and the ancient olive grove has been replaced with new trees planted closely together and growing well. There are no more winnowing forks or shocks of straw, nor any of those summer implements which brought the threshing floor to life. Their names are hardly known now. In less time than it takes a cockerel to sing out, the combine harvesters can clear a field of wheat, leaving neither stalk nor spike. But with combine harvesters singing is difficult.

There are many abandoned and decaying farmhouses. The land has become more solitary, the wild grasses have names now for the implacable herbicides; bees and bee-eaters seek refuge where they can against common enemies. Stony hillsides are more than ever places where beauty gathers and liberty reigns; shrub oaks have become holm oaks and wait expectantly for spring. Swallows, swifts and doves continue circling and nesting in neglected olive trees or the roofs of abandoned farmhouses.

But the countryside brings forth unending hidden splendours, accumulates them, renews them, and freely offers them to the eyes and the souls of those who wish to enjoy them. It makes clear in its restful silence that only by returning there will men encounter the best of themselves.

Alas, for those who forget this!

I began this book by saying, 'I know something of this land and its people'. Today I would say, 'I would like to know something of this land and its people.' It is worth adding this correction. One also learns from change and the passing years.

AUTHOR'S AFTERWORD, 1999
Published as 'Nota justificativa de la presente edición' in
Las cosas del campo. *Valencia-Buenos Aires: Pre-Textos 1999.*

The writing of this journal in 1946 and 1947 came about by chance. It was the result of having to fill the blank pages of a leather-bound book with paper dating from the eighteenth century which my older brother Juan had given me for this purpose. I wrote in pen straight out on whatever was occurring day by day in the Casería del Conde where I was then living, having married recently, in 1944. Now, re-reading the text for the present edition, I find that, rather than a diary of events in the countryside, it is more like a succession of brief notes which might have served for texts of greater length. The manuscript which I have kept contains many dates for individual entries, the whole following an order which is vaguely chronological and by season. The first date entered is 30 March 1946 and the last 21 May 1947, so that it covers the full cycle of the farm worker's year.

The manuscript remained unpublished for some years until, around 1950, my friends from Málaga, Pepe Salas, Bernabé Fernández Canivell and Alfonso Canales, who were at that time publishing an excellent poetry collection under the title *Arroyo de los Ángeles*, asked me if I could contribute to the series. I had nothing ready and could only offer them some prose texts on the countryside which I had been working on recently. My friends accepted this suggestion and the editing was entrusted to Bernabé who, as with all his work, did a most excellent job. An edition of 200 was made, mostly intended as gifts.

But that was not the end of the story, copies found their way into hands which considered the edition too small and so it was that the publishers Insula and their editor José Luis Cano (who today, as I write these lines, I remember with gratitude and admiration) published a new edition, corrected and augmented, of 1,000 copies which are today as impossible to come across as the first edition.

In this way *Las cosas del campo* became a book impossible to find until, around 1975, at the instigation of the publishers Destino and my friend Elena Quiroga, there was a new edition, which included *Las Musarañas*, published first in the *Revista del Occidente* in 1975, and *Las Sombras,* unpublished at that time. The last copies of that edition ended up on the bookstalls of the Cuesta de Moyano [in Madrid] where my friends and I acquired many of them for gifts. The present edition includes some unpublished texts.

TRANSLATORS' NOTE

The translators acknowledge the help provided by Pilar Fernández Martínez, *El mundo rural a través del léxico de José Antonio Muñoz Rojas,* Revista de estudios culturales, Universitat Jaume I, Barcelona 2013 vol XI, pp.67-81.

BIOGRAPHICAL NOTES

ANDREW DEMPSEY's books include three devoted to the photographs of the Mexican writer Juan Rulfo (RM editorial and Círculo de Arte); *A Life of Lorca: drawings, photographs, words* (University of East Anglia); *Sculptors Talking: Caro, Chillida* (Art of This Century); *The Three Mayors of Setenil* (Jacinas Press); and, as translator, Luis Cernuda, *Ocnos* (Turner, Colección Itálica).

ÁLVARO GARCÍA is a poet, novelist, translator and songwriter. He won the Hiperión poetry prize for *La noche junto al álbum*, 1989, and Loewe Prize for *Canción en blanco*, 2012. His most recent poetry collection is *Cuando hable el gato* published by Pre-Textos in 2023. He has written three novels, *El tenista argentino*, 2018, *Discurso de boda*, 2020, and *Elenco*, 2022. He has also written lyrics for *Ser sin sitio*, 2018, and *La única mañana*, 2023, by the musician Conde. His translations include Kipling, Eliot, Auden, Larkin, Margaret Atwood and Kenneth White.

www.ingramcontent.com/pod-product-compliance
Lightning Source LLC
Chambersburg PA
CBHW031634160426
43196CB00006B/407